ALL THE QUR'AN

in 100 pages

by a non-Muslim for non-Muslims

Amédée Turner

To Debby

Contents

Preface

Everything that is actually in the Qur'an is described in this book by a non-Muslim Westerner for non-Muslim readers. The descriptions are illustrated and underpinned with 400 most telling quotations. The book includes a special study of the relationship of the beheadings carried out by ISIS (Islamic State) in Syria) and Iraq to the provisions of the Qur'an. Everything that is actually and undeniably in the Qur'an is incontestable in Islam. However, all other Muslim writings are debated among Muslims, and none, outside the Qur'an remain uncontested by some branch of Muslims. The book has been deliberately kept as concise as possible and has been written as a non-erudite description of the Qur'an, being addressed to ordinary non-Muslims living in the West. Each Section has a completely illustrative collections of quotations from the relevant parts of the Qur'an, but a reader need only look at enough of each of these to confirm to his/her satisfaction that the message has been "got" on the point in question. Where to "skip" in this way, is indicated in the text. This book has been seen by a number of learned Muslims and their recommendations have been included.

The author, Amédée Turner is a Barrister, an English Queen's Counsel, was a member of the Advisory Council to the Anglican Observer mission to the United Nations from 2002 to 2006, and a Member of the European Parliament from 1979 to 1994. He is also carrying out studies, together with Dr. Davide Tacchini of Turin, on the attitudes of lay Muslims living in the West to the issue of Islam and democracy. These studies showed a general insistence that in a Muslim democracy "nothing contrary to the Qur'an shall happen". This underlines the desirability of some knowledge of the Qur'an by non-Muslims in the West. Amédée Turner would particularly welcome comments for guidance in improving this book. Please send any comments by email to: amedee.turner@btinternet.com

See also: http://www.muslim-grass-roots-discuss-democracy.com and https://en.wikipedia.org/wiki/Amédée_Turner

Acknowledgements

Editorial help: Penny Bridgers.
Typescript: Gloria Balbastro.
Arabic language advice: Aditi Jha

1:   The Nature of the Qur'an

It would be fruitless for a non-Muslim to attempt to evaluate the religious aspects of the Qur'an and an impertinence to attempt to appreciate its full Islamic light. It is also impossible for a non-Muslim to feel the spiritual effect, and poetry, of its Arabic language for an Arabic-speaking Muslim. But less than half the Muslim world is Arabic-speaking.

From a Western viewpoint, the Qur'an can seem to be a large collection of frequently repeated normally short messages, each recurring haphazardly again and again throughout the Book, sometimes with differing amounts of elaboration, but often with none. The wording often varies only slightly with each repetition. These, when sorted out, subject by subject, build up into the major issues addressed by the Qur'an and are presented, sorted out for a Westerner in the sections below. In addition there are a number of striking sentences of significance but without context which each occur only once or twice in the Qur'an. But as these are not enlarged on in the Qur'an they are collected together in Section 31 below.

2:   The origins of Islam and the Qur'an

Though in non-Islamic critiques there are doubts expressed about the provenance of the Qur'an, for instance the possibility that Muhammad must have been well cognisant of the two nearby great civilisations, the Christians of Byzantium and the Sasanium empire of Baghdad. Yet some curiously unfamiliar stories (totally without any religious significance) told in the Qur'an of Jesus and his mother suggest that Muhammad's contacts with Christians may indeed not have been with a sophisticated mainstream of Christianity, but with remote tribes of Christians in the desert on the outer borders of Christendom.

Whatever the actual situation of the origination of Qur'an, wherever and whenever that was, Islam was undeniably well-grounded and flourishing by 691 when the Dome of the Rock was built in Jerusalem, 59 years after the supposed date of Muhammad's death, and was decorated with many Muslim illustrations and Qur'anic quotations. This is a pretty speedy development, indicating a giant stride of some sort in the 7th century AD, 300 years after Christianity became spread widely in the Mediterranean world.

It is not clear why the Qur'anic quotations in the Dome of the Rock are not altogether identical with the currently accepted text of the Qur'an.

3: What is not in the Qur'an

Of significance are the things which are not to be found in the Qur'an, for instance punishment by stoning for any crime, and other punishments for crimes, now regarded by many Muslims as Islamic, but which were not designated in the Qur'an.

The many hundreds of thousands of ahadith ("traditions") recorded over the early centuries of Islam (starting with the earliest ahadith which are accepted by Muslims as being words of Muhammad), are, unlike the Qur'an itself, not taken to be the words of God. They are statements over which many different schools of Islamic thought have disagreed for more than 14 hundred years both as to authenticity and interpretation. Similarly, the many versions of Sharia law, originating after Muhammad's death, are disagreed over.

Thus in Islam only the Qur'an, which is the words of God, is accepted without question, although interpretation of these words is naturally subject to debate.

The Qur'an is quite unlike the Old Testament because it is not made up of stand-alone discourses and histories, and it is totally unlike the New Testament as it does not present a coherent history of the start of a religious movement.

4: The Purpose of this Book

This book is a guide by a non-Muslim for non-Muslims to the subjects addressed in the Qur'an upon which the tenets of Islam are built. For this purpose the numerous scattered (and repetitious) statements on each subject have been brought together so that the whole message on each can be seen in its completeness.

However sentiments concerning, *inter alia*, the beauty of the earth and the skies, which are common human sentiments, are not set out in this book. Though these sentiments (common to Christianity and indeed humankind) are excluded in the quotations below, it must be stressed that they play an essential role in Muslim thought. Thus the totality of the message of Islam includes much that is common to Christianity and other religions; however, only the message unique to Islam is described in this book.

The Qur'an relates all creation, the beauty of the earth and the sky to the purpose of God. This sentiment is particularly important to Muslims.

> 'There truly are signs in the creation of the heavens and earth, and in the alternation of night and day, for those with understanding, who remember God standing, sitting and lying down, who reflect on the creation of the heavens and earth. "Our Lord! You have not created all this without purpose - You are far above that!" (Med. 3/190).

> 'People, be mindful of your Lord, who created you from a single soul, and from it created its mate, and from the pair of them spread countless men and women far and wide, ... (Med. 4/1).

The purpose of God is indicated:

> 'I created jinn and mankind only to worship Me; ... (Mec. 51/56).

"Worship" implies submission of one's own will to God's, according to learned Muslim advice given to the author.

5: Use and Mal-use of the Qur'an

The actual wording in the Qur'an is notably relatively neutral as regards reflecting the aggressiveness or pacivity of Islam; but the wording is equally open to interpretation either along extremely aggressive lines on the one hand or along very pacific and mild lines on the other, with every gradation in between. Thus, ISIS (Islamic State) justifies the execution and slavery of thousands of Yazidis, Christians and Shiite Muslims by reliance on the wording of the Qur'an, just as on the other hand other present-day Muslims justify a wholly intellectual non-violent version of Islam. This book follows the middle course relying on the actual wording of the Qur'an, giving the wording throughout its most natural, unforced meaning.

At the time the Qur'an was received, fighting had only been experienced by the Muslims against a particular enemy, the polytheistic Meccans from Mecca, who had in the first instance attacked Muhammad's Muslims in Medina, and it is in this context that the statements about war and fighting according to the actual wording can only most naturally be considered.

But attention will be fully focused on more enforced interpretations including those of ISIS.

6: The Major Themes in the Qur'an

The major messages in the Qur'an that will strike a non-Muslim are concerned with a number of issues:

- the division of humankind into believers and disbelievers;
- the rewards of Paradise;
- the punishments of Hell;
- the rules for living a responsible life paying what one owes to society;
- the practicalities of governing the town of Medina in a time of war;

A large number of crimes and forbidden acts are designated only for punishment in Hell, but there are a very few forbidden acts for which punishments on earth are prescribed. Indeed the paucity of crimes for which punishment on earth is prescribed should be perhaps an important pragmatic message in the Qur'an. Above all is the absolute insistence on the reality of life after death.

The varying recurrence of repetitious statements on each subject naturally affects the weight of the over-all message given to each. This has been generally reflected in the extracts below. The various messages and repetitions in the Qur'an were understood to have been received by Muhammad directly from God's angelic messages over more than twenty years.

An extraordinarily large part of the text, about a quarter of the Qur'an, consists of parallels with Old Testament Bible stories concerning the destruction of wicked cities and their inhabitants associated with the lives of Abraham, Joseph, Lot, Noah, Moses and other Israelite leaders. These, although they take up the largest part of the whole text, are not represented below because the basic stories are known to non-Muslims in the West and do not indeed seem to modify the message, except for the stress they lay on the punishment by God for sin, not of individuals but of whole cities as found in the Old Testament.

The Qur'an adds many details to these Old Testament stories which are not found in the Old Testament, and whose sources are unverified by independent scholarship. Their significance appears to be in demonstrating how in the past history of humankind God had frequently destroyed all the inhabitants of sinful towns after they had rejected messengers sent to warn them to repent.

As to the New Testament, some of the few references to events, notably in the life of Jesus, appear extremely odd, and their sources and purpose are obscure to non-Muslims. It would seem possible that, quite apart from the basic concepts of Christianity there may have existed among local Christians in the desert in the near east where perhaps Muhammad lived, traditions which were far removed from the mainstream Christianity in the Roman Empire of the seventh century A.D.

7:   The Structure of the Qur'an

The Qur'an is divided into sections called suras and these into verses, and in the currently recognised texts, the suras are set out approximately in order of their length, the first and longest of about 30 pages, and the last and shortest, of three sentences in Arabic, one sentence in English.

However it is essential to be aware of when a particular sura was understood to have been received by Muhammad (in a revelation from God). Notably it must be appreciated whether a sura is regarded as being relatively early, having been received by Muhammad during the time he is considered to have been living in Mecca, where he had grown up, relatively peacefully, but largely unacknowledged, spurned or ridiculed by his fellow Meccans as an implausible prophet. Or whether a sura is considered to have been received from God later, from the time when Muhammad was said to have fled with a number of followers to Medina, 230 miles north, and was governing there while the town was under attack from the polytheist Meccans.

Each sura is identified as coming to him in the town of Mecca or in the town of Medina. Thus the Meccan suras show a prophet attempting, mostly unsuccessfully, to convert his fellow townspeople to a new view of religion, incidentally convincingly bearing out Jesus' own complaint that a prophet is not without honour save in his own country. Muhammad cites his fellow Meccans' attitude to him:

> 'The disbelievers say, "Do not listen to this Qur'an; drown it in frivolous talk .... " (Mec. 41/26).

> 'The disbelievers almost strike you down with their looks when they hear the Qur'an. They say, "He must be mad!" (Mec. 68/51).

However the Medinan suras show Muhammad in a very different situation; he was seen as governing a population principally of his own Muslim emigrant supporters who were said to have fled from Mecca with

5

him, or joined him later, many of whom had converted to Islam, as well as Jews and Christians already living in Medina. Muhammad was seen as having driven out the Jews. The Medinan suras indicate a leader in charge of a seventh century desert town dealing with all the political, military and social problems in a time of war. He ruled absolutely through his strength of character, but was constantly undermined by disrespectful citizens who made fun of him behind his back even though originally they had all presumably fled to Medina from Mecca to become Muslims led by him.

In each group of quotations from the Qur'an which are set out below, the Meccan quotations are put first and the Medinan second. A difference in tone between the Meccan suras and the Medinan suras will be clearly apparent. In the Meccan suras the revelations frequently attempt to convince Meccans of the need to adopt pure monotheism, because many Meccans were said to have been polytheists; in the Medinan suras Mohammad is rallying the town to fight for its survival against the besieging Meccans.

In the Meccan suras, Muhammad is shown as a native of Mecca and as scorned and treated as an outsider. The Medinan suras are much concerned with the practical matters of ordering life in Medina for the Meccan emigrants living in Medina, governing the town and conducting a defensive war against the invading Meccan enemy. In Medina he is shown as being in charge, though at times he indicates trepidation over his ability to maintain control of his followers, who make fun of him and disobey. Thus the Meccan suras are relatively 'mild' and the Medinan suras are relatively 'robust'. In Medina:–

> 'Some of the people listen to you (Prophet), but, once they leave your presence, they sneer at those who have been given knowledge, saying, 'what was that he just said?' (Med. 47/16)

> '... – say, "carry on with your jokes. ..." ' – yet if you were to question them, they would be sure to say, "We were just chatting, just amusing ourselves." Say, "Were you joking about God, His Revelation and His Messenger (i.e., Muhammad)? Do not try to justify yourselves; you have gone from belief to disbelief." (Med. 9/64)

8: The Make-up of the Qur'an

There are 87 Meccan suras having more than 4100 verses, amounting to approximately 55% of the total content of the book, and 27 Medinan suras of more than 1600 verses amounting to approximately 45% of the total. Thus

6

the Meccan suras and the verses making them up tend to be on average only one third the length of the Medinan. As the suras are set out approximately simply in order of their *length*, the Meccan and Medinan suras are mixed up haphazardly. The first known written version of the Qur'an dates from the early 8th century, that is sometime after the quotations from the Qur'an were set up in the Dome of the Rock in Jerusalem, as mentioned above, in 691.

In fact, on looking at a translation of the Qur'an it may very well be appealing to a non-Muslim reader to read from the back to the front, thus getting the shorter messages first, or better still to do this, but first reading all the (earlier) Meccan suras from the back, then similarly the (later) Medinan. The Qur'an is half the length of the New Testament and is a one seventh of the length of the Old Testament. But it is impossible usefully to select a particular illustrative part to read because, as mentioned above, each subject is reverted to again and again throughout the Book.

The proportion of space given to each subject in the selections below approximately reflects the proportion which that subject is given in the Qur'an.

The quotations below are identified as being Meccan "(Mec.)" or Medinan "(Med.)" with the sura number followed by the verse number.

9:   The Content of the Qur'an

Two substantial messages of the Qur'an are not represented below because they do not significantly illustrate the distinctive aspects of Islam. First there are a considerable number of short descriptions of the world, the skies or heavens, and of the bounty of the earth as the gifts of God, and of the creation of humankind by God. They are not calculated to influence human behaviour beyond creating awe and gratitude for God's gifts to mankind.

Secondly, as mentioned above, one quarter of all the verses in the Qur'an comprise repeated and often long descriptions of God's destruction of Old Testament cities, by fire, brimstone or flood, because of the sinfulness of their inhabitants and their rejection of God's messengers. These parts of the Qur'an are not represented in the quotations set out below, but it should be kept in mind what a considerable portion of the Qur'an is comprised of them. Also not represented below are over a hundred references to God's punishment and destruction of sinful and disbelieving towns in past history not found in the Old Testament but presumably known to Muhammad's contemporaries.

By far the greatest impact of the Qur'an to an outsider is in the number of warnings, often with horrific details, in dire terms, of the consequences of disbelief and sin: nearly 350 explicit references to the punishments and the horrors awaiting Muhammad's contemporary Arabs who were refusing to believe in the existence of a next life and who were therefore to be consigned to Hell on the Day of Resurrection (indeed with all other races of men who refused to believe). There is nearly one threat per page in the Meccan sections. This message is fully represented in the extracts below.

It is quite clear in the text of the Qu'ran that Muhammad's opponents were confident that there was no after-life for humankind and no resurrection, and that an individual's death ended all things for that person, and that therefore there were no further consequences from a person's behaviour on earth.

'They say, "There is only our life in this world: we die, we live, nothing but time destroys us". They have no knowledge of this; they only follow guesswork. Their only argument, when Our (God's) clear revelations are recited to them, is to say, "Bring back our forefathers if what you say is true". (Mec. 45/24).

It might be interesting to enquire what, if any, effect an alleged increase in this attitude in Western life in the twentieth and twenty-first centuries is having on current human behaviour in the West.

Next in significance, is the idyllic existence in the next life for those who in this life believe and do not sin, or who repent of their sins, - again commencing on the Day of Resurrection when they will enter Paradise, in "Gardens graced with flowing streams" described repeatedly in lyrical terms. There are mentions of "maidens", yes, (but never a mention, precisely, of "seventy two", "seventy" or even "seven" virgins). However these are described only a third as frequently (120 times) as are the pains of Hell.

After this in order of length come about eighty descriptions of crimes and forbidden acts and rules for living, then about fifty passages diversely on women, children and slaves.

It is politically particularly significant that there are forty or more occasions when, while in describing Muhammad ruling Medina in the war, Muhammad's instructions to the people cite not just God, but Muhammad himself jointly with God: "God and His Messenger" ("His Messenger" being Muhammad) as being the authority for instructing the Medinans what is needed from them to organise and fight off the Meccans in the war against Mecca.

The statistics given in this book are as accurate as possible but may be a few percentage points out. The references to verse numbers may call for looking in the text of the Qur'an at the verses just before or just after the number given, as many references straddle a number of verses.

The translation used is that of the Oxford University Press, 2004, 2010, by Professor M.A.S. Abdel Haleem of Al Azhar, Cairo and Cambridge Universities and the School of Oriental and African Studies, University of London. Needless to say any translation loses the ethereality felt by Muslims of the Arabic text; and this particular translation is very down-to-earth in its expression.

Of course there are many ways in which a Muslim reads the Qur'an (as there are of Christians reading the Bible) but when scholarly exercises go into exegesis they are naturally explorations beyond the plain text of the Qur'an. Such exegesis and extrapolations are found in the many hundreds of thousands of ahadith, being later developments out of the Qur'an, and reflecting different denominations of Islam, such as Sunni, Shia and Sufi. But this book is only concerned with the presently accepted 7th century Qur'an itself.

P.S. a devout Muslim wished to contribute a modern gloss to this book standing back from the apparently haphazard compilation of messages in the Qur'an. She contributed this view of Islam, "There is such a thing as a Divine Being (al-lah = the Almighty), that 'He' is beyond our ability to comprehend except as He reveals, that He is the guide and intimate lover of souls, whether they turn to Him or turn away, and is forgiver and compassionate, knowing all circumstances etc. The key qualities are faith, acceptance of God's almighty wisdom, the acceptance of life beyond death and our placement in it, angelic guidance, and such qualities as modesty, gentleness, courage, honesty, generosity, and so on." This will immediately be recognised as exemplary of one of the pacific as distinct from the more aggressive readings.

10:   The Origin and Reception of the Qur'an

The origination of the Qur'an is described in three Meccan verses.

'The Qur'an is nothing less than a revelation that is sent to him (Muhammad). It was taught to him by (an angel) with mighty powers and great strength who stood on the highest horizon and then approached – coming down until he was two bow lengths away or even closer – and revealed to God's servant what He revealed. (Mec. 53/4).

'You (Prophet), (Muhammad), enfolded in your cloak! Stay up throughout the night, all but a small part of it, half, or a little less, or a little more; recite the Qur'an slowly and distinctly; We (God) shall send a momentous message down to you. (Mec. 73/1).

These two quotations both show an amusing vagueness over distance and time!

'You (Muhammad), wrapped in your cloak, arise and give warning! Proclaim the greatness of your Lord: cleanse yourself; keep away from all filth; do not be overwhelmed and weaken, be steadfast in your Lord's cause. (Mec. 74/1).

'It (the Qur'an) is a recitation that We (God) have revealed in parts, so that you (Muhammad) can recite it to people at intervals. We (God) have sent it down little by little. (Mec. 17/106).

'Some say, "Muddled dreams", others, "He has made it up!" yet others, "He is just a poet, let him show us a sign as previous messengers did." (Mec. 21/5).

They say "Receiver of this Qur'an! You are definitely mad." (Mec. 15/6).

11:   The Completeness of the Qur'an

'We (God) have sent the Scripture down to you explaining everything, (Mec. 16/89).

'We (God) have missed nothing out of the Record. (Mec. 6/38).

However it is stated also that:

'When We (God) substitute one revelation for another – and God knows best what He reveals – they say, "You are just making it up", but most of them have no knowledge. (Mec. 16/101).

Some of its verses are definite in meaning – they are the cornerstone of the Scripture – and others are ambiguous.

> 'The perverse at heart eagerly pursue the ambiguities in their attempt to make trouble and to pin down a specific meaning of their own: only God knows the true meaning. (Med. 3/7).

> 'Any revelation We (God) cause to be superseded or forgotten, We (God) replace with something better or similar. (Med. 2/106).

> 'God erases or confirms whatever He will, and the source of Scripture is with Him. (Med. 13/39).

The literal contents of the Qur'an itself are considered by Muslims to be the humanly unmediated word of God and, therefore are, naturally, indisputable.

In contrast, the contents of the Bible, Old and New Testaments, do not have this unchallengeable status because (except possibly among certain fundamentalist church sects) the Bible though, the "word of God", is considered to have been humanly-mediated.

Subsequent Islamic thought in the following millennium and a half, notably the various forms of Sharia and many hundreds of thousands of ahadith have developed in a number of very different schools of thought giving rise to many long-standing and basic differences of opinion, from the most war-like to the most pacific.

In addition Med. 2/106 quoted last but one above has been taken to give scope for later scholars and clerics to "abrogate" earlier Meccan (and more pacific) verses by later Medinan (and more aggressive) verses, where they can claim that a contradiction exists. This controversial procedure cannot safely be indulged in by non-Muslims. Furthermore no specific abrogation and substitution is to be found anywhere in the Qur'an itself.

12:   Muslim Interpretations of the Qur'an

Reformist and conservative Muslims today will interpret the Qur'an in the light of subsequent scholarly and religious thought and present-day concepts of what is or is not appropriate, – or in some cases in extremist directions. A remarkable example of the reformist trend is Professor Tariq Ramadan of Oxford University's example (in "What I Believe", OUP, 2010, page 3). He deliberately takes up a difficult case; he refers to Medinan sura 4, verse 34 which states that a husband shall (note: it is "shall", not "may") hit his wife if he fears high-handedness from her.

This has naturally caused concern going back far in Muslim scholarship and has led to a large number of different glosses. Tariq Ramadan states that his procedure is that he takes the "most literalist" meaning of the original Qur'anic verse to the most reformist, "which read this verse in light of the global message and contextualise the verse ... as well as taking their chronology into account. In the light of those interpretations and considering the example set by the Prophet, who never struck a woman, I say that domestic violence contradicts Islamic teachings and that such behaviour is to be condemned."

This is fine and comforting, and most non-Muslims would agree with the sentiment; but a Muslim of different views may equally well take a statement in the Qur'an relating to war (where the literal terms only countenance defensive fighting in the specific context of the war between the Meccans and Medinans), and claim to "contextualise the verse" by concluding that aggression of the most general and terroristic nature correctly "contextualises the verse".

Ramadan's "interpretation" also seems to regard the Qur'an as a document with 7th century limitations. But it is the timeless word of God.

For non-Muslims the only conclusion can be that we take the Qur'an as it stands. Non-Muslims will find no difficulty in applying contemporary attitudes to the original seventh century text, as the great majority of them equally do to what are considered to be superseded concepts in the Old, and in some cases the New, Testament Bible.

As mentioned above, such a procedure is less fraught for Christians with regard to the Bible, because the Bible is not the direct word of God. Thus they may say "hitting a wife was accepted in the 7th century context, but it is not accepted by us now." This evasion is not open to Muslims for whom the Qur'an is the direct and immutable word of God. But in the centuries since the 7th century many elaborate methods of interpretation have developed in different and often totally contradictory directions.

Non-Muslims cannot with any confidence choose between these, so this book confines itself to the actual words of the Qur'an.

13: Ways for Non-Muslims to Interpret the Qur'an

Those in the West have, since the rise of ISIS (Islamic State in Iraq and Syria) become more aware of the extreme differences of "interpretation" of the Qur'an that are possible in Muslim thinking. ISIS justifies its mass executions by beheading and other means by direct reference to the Qur'an, just as do peaceable Muslims, such as Tariq Ramadan with his definition of striking a wife described above.

Westerners can "take sides" and follow interpretations with extreme violence or those with extreme "gentleness", but either route would lead them to conclusions which would not be generally warrantable. Undoubtedly, in the political world, of the rise of ISIS, non-Muslims must retain the right to read injunctions in the Qur'an as reflecting both extremely violent and extremely pacifist points of view. This is only prudent in preparing oneself for all possible eventualities.

However for the Westerner in arriving at conclusions as to the nature of Islam as a principle of life, a philosophy, it is only justifiable to take the actual words of the Qur'an at their face value. That is what this book attempts to do.

14: Old Testament Destruction of Sinful Biblical Cities

Because, as already mentioned, the stories from the Old Testament of the destruction of wicked cities take up the largest space, a quarter, of the Qur'an, reference must be made to them again, here, simply because of their predominance. It may be added that there can be found some truly remarkable additions to these Old Testament stories.

> 'We (God) relate to you, (Muhammad), such accounts of earlier towns:
> some of them are still standing; some have been mown down; We did
> not wrong them; they wronged themselves.(Mec. 11/100).

There are 130 separate descriptions of disasters which have been meted out to the wicked cities of the Old Testament. They amount to nearly 1400 verses. They all rehearse the punishment visited on cities and communities in the stories of prophets and messengers of the Old Testament whose message was rejected. Most frequently these relate to Abraham, Lot, Moses and Noah. Though not calculated, it is probable that these Old Testament references make 200–300 references to the same, perhaps ten, limited number of catastrophic Old Testament events.

'When We (God) decide to destroy a town, We command those corrupted by wealth (to reform), but they (persist in their) disobedience; Our sentence is passed, and We destroy them utterly. (Mec. 17/16).

15:   The Day of Resurrection

The Day of Resurrection must be mentioned second as it is central to both the punishment for disbelievers and sinners and the blessings for believers and those who do good, and can almost never be out of the mind of the reader of the Qur'an.

It cannot be overstressed that belief in the after-life is a, or rather *the sine qua non* of the Qur'an.

'As for those who do not believe in the life to come, We have made their deeds seem alluring to them, so they will wander blindly; it is they who will have the worst suffering. (Mec. 27/4)

There are, it must be stressed, only two categories of people given consideration in the Qur'an: those rewarded or those condemned on the Day of Resurrection, according to how they have lived their lives. Those who believe and do good rest forever in the "Gardens", while disbelievers and sinners are condemned to the endless torments of Hell. There are slight suggestions that these torments might not necessarily continue *for ever*.

'These people have no grasp of God's true measure. On the Day of Resurrection the whole earth will be in His grip. The heavens will be rolled up in His right hand – Glory be to Him! … (Mec. 39/67).

'… the Trumpet will be sounded, and everyone in the heavens and earth will fall down senseless except those God spares. It will be sounded once again and they will be on their feet, looking on. The earth will shine with the Light of its Lord; the Record of Deeds will be laid open; the prophets and witnesses will be brought in. Fair judgement will be given between them: they will not be wronged and every soul will be repaid in full for what it has done. He (God) knows best what they do. (Mec. 39/68).

'Those who rejected the Truth will be led to Hell in their throngs. When they arrive, its gates will open and its keepers will say to them, "Were you not sent your own messengers to recite the revelations of your Lord to you and warn you that you would meet this Day?" and they will say, "Yes, indeed we were." But the sentence of punishment will have been passed against those who rejected the truth. It will be said, "Enter the gates of Hell: there you will remain. How evil is the abode of the arrogant!" (Mec. 39/71).

'Those who were mindful of their Lord will be led in throngs to the Garden. When they arrive, they will find its gates wide open, and its keepers will say to them, "Peace be upon you. You have been good. Come in: you are here to stay," and they will say, "Praise be to God who has kept His promise to us and given us this land as our own. Now we may live wherever we please in the Garden." How excellent is the reward of those who labour! You (Prophet) will see the angels surrounding the Throne, glorifying their Lord with praise. True judgment will have been passed between them, and it will be said, "Praise be to God, the Lord of the Worlds." (Mec. 39/73).

16: Punishment in Hell

It cannot be denied that punishment for an individual's sin (*in addition* to that accorded to the wicked ancient cities), word for word and verse for verse, occupies the greater part of the text of the Qur'an. But it should be borne in mind that this is punishment in Hell on the Day of Resurrection, not punishment on earth. Punishment in Hell is taken up on three hundred and fifty separate occasions, most often in multiple verses.

Generally these individual threats of the punishments of Hell on the Day of Resurrection are against "disbelievers" or "disbelievers and those who sin"; only on a very small minority of occasions are other specific sins referred to. A list of these is:

Usury, (Med. 2/275), distorting scripture, (Med. 2/78), fleeing battle in the Medinan war (Med. 8/16), consuming orphans' property, (Med. 4/10), blaming another for one's own sin, (Med. 4/112), rejecting the faith and denying revelations(i.e. apostasy), (Med. 5/10), idolatry, (Med. 9/17), hoarding gold and silver, (Med. 9/35), hypocrisy, (Med. 9/68,73,79), false accusations against Muhammad's wife A'isha, (Med. 24/23), People of the Book (Christians and Jews) who disbelieve, (Med. 98/6), whoever opposes God and His Messenger, (Med. 9/63), People of the Book (Jews and Christians) who broke faith (a treaty agreed by Muhammad with the Jews in Medina), (Med. 59/3). Whoever has done an atom's weight of evil, (Med. 99/7).

Drinking intoxicating liquids and gambling are specified sins, but punishment in Hell is not specifically designated for them, nor is there any punishment specified on earth.

> 'They ask you (Prophet) about intoxicants and gambling, say, "There is great sin in both, and some benefit for people: the sin is greater than the benefit". (Med. 2/219).

It has been said that the reference is strictly to "wine", not all intoxicants. But this is not usually relied on.

But the great mass of the victims of Hell, repeatedly cited, are simply "disbelievers" or "disbelievers and sinners".

Many of the descriptions of the punishments and torments of Hell, which are to last indefinitely after the Day of Resurrection are lurid and detailed; but in general punishment is described simply as "dreadful", "terrible" or "the Fire". But among these general references there are some specific and graphic descriptions of Hell:

> The reader can go to the next section when the message of these quotations is clear.

> 'Just one blast and – lo and behold! – they will look and say, "Woe to us! This is the Day of Judgment!" (Mec. 37/19).

> 'The wretched ones will be in the Fire, sighing and groaning, there to remain for as long as the heavens and earth endure, unless your Lord wills otherwise; ... (Mec. 11/106).

> '(The condemned) will be given foul water to drink, which he will try to gulp but scarcely be able to swallow; ... (Mec. 14/16).

> '... He (God) only gives them respite until a Day when their eyes will stare in terror. They will rush forward, craning their necks, unable to divert their eyes, a gaping void in their hearts. (Mec. 14/42).

> '... they will have boiling water to drink .... (Mec. 6/70).

> '... you (Prophet) will see the guilty on that Day, bound together in fetters, in garments of pitch, their faces covered in fire. (Mec. 14/49).

'We have prepared a Fire for the wrongdoers that will envelop them from all sides. If they call for relief they will be relieved with water like molten metal, scalding their faces. What a terrible drink! What a painful resting place! (Mec. 18/29).

'Hell will be the reward ..., there they will stay, neither living nor dying, ... (Mec. 20/74).

'We shall drag him by his forehead (this refers to sinful men in general) – his lying, sinful forehead ... . We shall summon the guards of Hell, ... (Mec. 96/15).

'Woe to every fault-finding backbiter who amasses riches, counting them over, thinking they will make him live for ever. No indeed! He will be thrust into the Crusher! (said to refer to a particular critic of Muhammad in Mecca). (Mec. 104/1).

'May the hands of Abu Lahab be ruined! May he be ruined too! Neither his wealth nor his gains will help him: he will burn in the flaming Fire – and so will his wife, the firewood-carrier, with a palm-fibre rope around her neck. (two individual tormenters of Muhammad in Mecca). (Mec. 111/1).

'If anything can amaze you (Prophet), then you should surely be amazed at their asking, "What? When we become dust, shall we be created anew?" These are the ones who deny their Lord, who will wear iron collars around their necks and be the inhabitants of the Fire, there to remain. (Med. 13/5).

Hell is decreed for those described as opponents of Muhammad in Medina who disbelieved in God:–

'Garments of fire will be tailored for those who disbelieve; scalding water will be poured over their heads, melting their insides as well as their skins; there will be iron crooks to restrain them: whenever, in their anguish, they try to escape, they will be pushed back in and told, "Taste the suffering of the Fire." (Med. 22/19).

'We have prepared a blazing Fire for those who do not believe in God and His Messenger. (Med. 48/13).

'Do they not know that whoever opposes God and His Messenger (Muhammad) will go to the Fire of Hell and stay there? That is the supreme disgrace. (Med. 9/63).

17: Punishment by God During Life on Earth

As mentioned above, reference to punishment in this life is almost exclusively not for individual sinners but as descriptions of catastrophes that have occurred, directed by God at whole cities and communities of the Old Testament. Most commonly these communities have rejected a prophet or messenger, rather as Mecca is said to have rejected Muhammad.

As distinct from punishment by the destruction of whole communities, there are *a very few occasions* when punishment during life on earth is indicated for an individual's sins. Examples are, (author's italics),

'Those who invent lies about God will not prosper. (*i.e., in this life*). (Mec. 10/69).

'… there are some who … lead others astray from God's path. *Disgrace in this world awaits such a person* … and, on the Day of Resurrection … the suffering of the Fire. (Med. 22/8).

'… no one can guide those God leaves to stray. There is a *punishment for them in this world*, but the punishment of the Hereafter will be harder – (Med. 13/33).

'… Those who accuse honourable but unwary believing women (in fact A'isha, Muhammad's wife) are rejected by God, *in this life* and the next. (Med. 24/23).

18: God does not seek to save wilful wrong-doers

There are very many promises that God forgives sinners, including disbelievers, if they repent, (and of course for disbelievers if they believe).

'(Whoever does these things (sins) will face the penalties: their torment will be doubled on the Day of Resurrection, and they will remain in torment, disgraced, except those who repent, believe, and do good deeds God will change the evil deeds of such people into good ones. He is most forgiving, most merciful. People who repent and do good deeds truly return to God). (Mec. 25/68).

'God loves those who do good – those who remember God and implore forgiveness for their sins if they do something shameful or wrong themselves – who forgives sins but God? – and who never knowingly persist in doing wrong. The reward for such people is forgiveness from their Lord, and Gardens graced with flowing streams ... (Med. 3/134).

'(Prophet), tell the disbelievers that if they desist their past will be forgiven. (Med. 8/38).

The responsibility of each person for his/her own acts is very clear in the Qur'an, and it must be said that there is no indication that God seeks out wilful sinners to save them in the manner of the good shepherd and the search for the lost sheep as described in the New Testament and frequently painted in the early Christian catacombs. In fact it must be said, – it just cannot be denied – amazingly – that some people are deliberately left to go astray by God. This may be the most startling aspect of the Qur'an. It may be possible to imply that God gives sinners and disbelievers the express choice of repenting but this is mostly certainly not expressed in the following quotations.

This is an extraordinary difference from the New Testament and may go to the root of the distinctiveness of Islam.

> The reader can go to the next section when the message of these quotations is clear. Nonetheless the message of the whole is very compelling.

'If God allows someone to stray he has no one to guide him. If God guides someone no one can lead him astray. (Mec. 39/36).

'Anyone God allows to stray will have no one else to protect him. (Mec. 42/44).

'If God so willed, he would have made you all one people, but He leaves some to stray whoever He will and guides whoever He will. (Mec. 16/93).

'God leaves whoever He will to stray and guides whoever He will. (Mec. 74/31).

'Who can guide those God leaves to stray? ... (Mec. 30/29).

'God does not guide the wrong-doers. (Mec. 61/7).

'Whoever follows the right path follows it for his own good, and whoever strays does so to his own loss. I (Muhammad) am not your guardian.
(Mec. 10/108).

'But if they turn away (Prophet), your only duty is to deliver the message clearly. (Mec. 16/82).

'God points out the right path, for some paths lead the wrong way: if He wished, He could guide you all. (Mec. 16/9).

'Now the truth has come from your Lord: let those who wish to believe in it do so, and let those who wish to reject it do so. (Mec. 18/29).

'As for those who refuse to do this (to direct themselves wholly to God) ... they will return to Us and We (God) shall tell them what they have done: God knows all that hearts contain. – We let them enjoy themselves for a little while, but We shall drive them to harsh torment. (Mec. 31/23).

'God does not guide those who reject Him. These are people whose hearts, hearing and sight have been closed off *by God* (author's italics); they are heedless, and there is no doubt that they will be the losers in the Hereafter. (Mec. 16/107).

'Alas for those whose hearts harden at the mention of God! They have clearly lost their way. God has sent down the most beautiful of all teachings: a Scripture that is consistent and draws comparisons; that causes the skins of those in awe of their Lord to quiver. Then their skins and their hearts soften at the mention of God: such is God's guidance. He guides with it whoever He will; no one can guide those God leaves to stray. (Mec. 39/22).

'Even if We (God) sent the angels down to them, and the dead spoke to them, and We gathered all things right in front of them, they still would not believe, unless God so willed .... (Mec. 6/111).

'If God so willed, He would have made you all one people, but he leaves to stray whoever he will and guides whoever he will. (Mec. 16/93).

'If God leaves someone to stray, you (Prophet) will never find a way for him. (Med. 4/143).

'God does not guide those who break away. (Med. 9/24).

'Misfortunes can only happen with God's permission – He will guide the heart of anyone who believes in Him: God knows all things – so obey God and the Messenger. If you turn away, remember that Our Messenger's (Muhammad's) duty is only to make plain his message. (Med. 64/11).

'God does not guide the wrongdoers. (Med. 61/7).

'Do you want to guide those God has left to stray? (Med. 4/88).

'We (God) send devils to incite the disbelievers to sin. (Mec. 19/83)

Along the same lines, but with added emphasis that God may decide who not to guide, are the following:

> Again, the reader can go to the next section when the message of these quotations is clear.

'Do you (Prophet) not see how We (God) set evil ones on the disbelievers to incite them? ... We (God) are counting down their (allotted) time. On the Day We gather the righteous as an honoured company ... and drive the sinful like a thirsty herd into Hell. (Mec. 19/83).

'Who could be more wrong than the person who is reminded of his Lord's messages and turns his back on them, ignoring what his hands are storing up for him (in the Hereafter)? We have put covers over their hearts, so they cannot understand the Qur'an ...; although you call them to guidance (Prophet) they will never accept it. (Mec.18/57)

'(Prophet), when you recite the Qur'an, We put an invisible barrier between you and those who do not believe in the life to come. We have put covers over their hearts that prevent them from understanding it, and a heaviness in their ears. When you mention your Lord in the Qur'an, and Him alone, they turn their backs and run away. (Mec. 17/45)

'This (Hell Fire) is what they will get for rejecting our signs and saying "What? When we are turned to bones and dust, how can we be raised in a new act of creation?" (Mec. 17/98).

'Even if they saw a piece of heaven falling down on them, they would say, "Just a heap of clouds," so leave them, Prophet, until they face the Day when they will be thunderstruck. (Mec. 52/44).

'They say, "What? Shall we be brought back to life, after we have turned into decayed bones?" And they say, "Such a return is impossible!" But all it will take is a single blast, and they will be (back) above ground. (Mec. 79/10).

'No one can guide those God allows to stray. He leaves them blundering about in their insolence. (Mec. 7/186).

'... God will not forgive those who have disbelieved and do evil, nor will He guide them to any path except that of Hell .... (Med. 4/168).

'If God intends some people to be so misguided, you (Muhammad) will be powerless against God on their behalf. These are the ones whose hearts God does not intend to cleanse – a disgrace for them in this world, and then a heavy punishment in the Hereafter. (Med. 5/41).

Predestination or not

Some of these quotations at face value indicate that God has predestined some people to continue sinning. They are probably not to be regarded as definite indications of predestination because there are many indications throughout the Qur'an that God welcomes back repentant sinners. These quotations should probably therefore not be regarded as indications of man's lack of freedom to decide his own fate. Nonetheless the stance is extreme. See also Section 29: Predestination, on page 78.

19: Rewards in Paradise

First it may be noted that mention of rewards during one's life on earth for good deeds are both rare and brief; thus:

'There is good in this present world for those who do good, but their home in the Hereafter is far better; the home of the righteous is excellent. (Mec. 16/30).

'... see how We (God) have given some more than others – but the Hereafter holds greater ranks and greater favours. (Mec. 17/21).

'There are some who pray, "Our Lord, give us good in this world;" and they will have no share in the Hereafter; others pray, "Our Lord give us good in this world and in the Hereafter, and protect us from the torment of the Fire." They will have the share they have worked for . . . (Med. 2/200).

The reward on the Day of Resurrection is practically always simply promised to "believers and those who do good deeds" and to those who have repented of their evil.

'People who repent and do good deeds truly return to God, (Mec. 25/71).

'We shall certainly blot out the misdeeds of those who believe and do good deeds, and we shall reward them according to the best of their actions.
(Mec. 29/7).

'(As for) those who avoid grave sins and foul acts, though they commit small sins, your Lord is ample in forgiveness.(Mec. 53/32).

'He (God) will overlook the faults of those who have faith, do good deeds, and believe in what has been sent down to Muhammad. (Med. 47/2).

'But if you avoid the great sins you have been forbidden, we shall wipe out your minor misdeeds and let you through the entrance of honour (to Paradise). (Med. 4/31).

There are, however, rare occasions when the reward on the Day of Resurrection is related to specific deeds. These are:

'Goodness does not consist in turning your face towards East or West. The truly good are those who believe in God and the Last Day, in the angels, the Scripture, and the prophets; who give away some of their wealth, however much they cherish it, to their relatives, to orphans, the needy, travellers and beggars, and to liberate those in bondage; those who keep up the prayer and pay the prescribed alms; who keep pledges whenever they make them; who are steadfast in misfortune, adversity, and times of danger. These are the ones who are true, and it is they who are aware of God. (Med. 2/177).

'... To anyone who fights in God's way, whether killed or victorious, We shall give a great reward. (Med. 4/74).

'... Whoever has done an atom's-weight of good, ... (Med. 99/7).

'... those who obey Him (God) and His Messenger, ... (Med. 4/13).

'... those who migrated in God's way and were killed or died, (following Muhammad from Mecca to Medina). (Med. 22/58).

'... (Christians) not given to arrogance, and when they listen to what has been sent down to the Messenger (Muhammad), you see their eyes overflowing with tears because they recognise the Truth (in it). (Med. 5/83).

The reward is to inhabit "Gardens graced with flowing streams." The reward is promised 96 times in Meccan suras and 55 times in Medinan suras. When the reward is not elaborated the references are not set out below; but when the description of the 'Gardens' is extended to further detail the most notable instances are the following:

'... Gardens of lasting bliss graced with flowing streams. There they will be adorned with bracelets of gold. There they will wear green garments of fine silk and brocade, ... comfortably seated on soft chairs. (Mec. 18/31).

'There they will remain, never wishing to leave (the Gardens of Paradise), ... (Mec. 18/108).

'There, they will hear only peaceful talk, nothing bad; there they will be given provision morning and evening, ... (Mec. 19/62).

'... so today the believers are laughing at the disbelievers as they sit on couches, gazing around. (Mec. 83/34).

Finally there are a considerable number of references to specific characteristics of society in Paradise (but, as mentioned above, not specifically 72, 70 or 7 virgins). It is however impossible not to notice that the descriptions are entirely male-oriented. Earthly wives and their standing in Paradise do not appear to be in contemplation. Despite this, it should be noted nonetheless that wives are specifically stated to enter Paradise with their husbands:

'... those who devoted themselves to Us. Enter Paradise, "you and your spouses ..." (Mec. 43/70).

Apart from this reference however the orientation is wholly male and not suggestive of married rather than other types of heavenly bliss.

Note: In one passage Muhammad sees Christians as entering Paradise (see quotation Med. 5/82 on page 50 below). But this is not so when the Christian Trinity is in consideration, see quotation Med. 5/72 also on page 51. It would seem that Muhammad knew of certain Christians who did not indicate (at any rate to him) belief in the Trinity.

> The reader can go to the next section when the message of these quotations is clear.

'They will have familiar provisions – fruits – and will be honoured in gardens of delight, seated on couches, facing one another. A drink will be passed round among them from a flowing spring: white, delicious to those who taste it, causing no headiness or intoxication. With them will be spouses – modest of gaze and beautiful of eye – like protected eggs. (Mec. 37/40). (Not a reference to their earthly spouses?)

'For these will be the ones brought nearest to God in Gardens of Bliss: many from the past and a few from later generations. On couches of well-woven cloth they will sit facing each other; everlasting youths will go round among them with glasses, flagons and cups of pure drink that causes no headache or intoxication; (there will be) any fruit they choose; the meat of any bird they like and beautiful-eyed maidens like hidden pearls; a reward for what they used to do. They will hear no idle or sinful talk there, only clean and wholesome speech ... they will dwell amid thornless lote trees and clustered acacia with spreading shade, constantly flowing water, abundant fruits, unfailing, unforbidden, with incomparable companions We have specially created – virginal, loving, of matching age. (Mec. 56/12).

So much for earthly wives and their heaven! Though it is stated, see above, in one sentence, that wives are countenanced in Paradise.

'Gardens of lasting bliss with gates wide open. They will be comfortably seated; they will call for abundant fruit and drink; they will have well-matched (wives) with modest gaze. (Mec. 38/50).

'... there is supreme fulfilment: gardens, vineyards, maidens of matching age and an overflowing cup. (Mec. 78/32).

'They are comfortably seated on couches arranged in rows; We pair them with beautiful-eyed maidens; We *unite the believers with their offspring who followed them in faith* ... We provide them with any fruit or meat they desire. They pass around a cup which does not lead to any idle talk or sin. Devoted youths like hidden pearls wait on them. They turn to one another and say, "When we were still with our families (on earth) we used to live in fear – but God has been gracious to us and saved us from the torment of intense heat. We used to pray to Him ...." (Mec. 52/20). (Author's italics)

It seems a little unexpected that with this description there could also be a reference to their earthly families, see italics.

'(Prophet), say, "Would you like me tell you of things that are better than all of these? Their Lord will give those who are mindful of God Gardens graced with flowing streams, where they will stay with pure spouses and God's good pleasure- God is fully aware of His servants ...." (Med. 3/15).

'... there are two gardens .... With shading branches .... With a pair of flowing springs .... With every kind of fruit in pairs .... They will sit on couches upholstered with brocade, the fruit of both gardens within easy reach .... There will be maidens restraining their glances, untouched beforehand by man or jinn .... Like rubies and brilliant pearls, ... There are two other gardens below these two .... Both of deepest green .... With a pair of gushing springs .... With fruits – date palms and pomegranate trees .... There are good-natured, beautiful maidens .... Dark-eyed, sheltered in pavilions .... Untouched beforehand by man or jinn .... They will sit on green cushions and fine carpets .... (Med. 55/46).

'They will sit on couches, feeling neither scorching heat not biting cold, with shady (branches) spread above them and clusters of fruit hanging close at hand. They will be served with silver plates and gleaming silver goblets according to their fancy, and they will be given a drink infused with ginger from a spring called Salsabil. Everlasting youths will attend them – if you could see them, you would think they were scattered pearls – and if you were to look around, you would see bliss and great opulence: they will wear garments of green silk and brocade; they will be adorned with silver bracelets; their Lord will give them a pure drink .... (Med. 76/13).

Note: The above is indeed the description of the rewards of Paradise found in the Qur'an and might be considered particularly surprising in the light of family love and unity particularly at the time of death. But a learned Muslim in reaction to the above quotations has advised the author of an entirely different priority, other than bliss in Paradise, and that it should also be said that the deeper message in the Qur'an as a whole is that the most important punishment of all is to be deprived of knowing God and of tasting His love; and that the greatest reward is to get close to the oneness of God.

Thus this learned Muslim lessens the Qur'an's message of Paradise.

20:   Everyday Rules For Living as a Muslim

The Qur'an naturally contains a considerable body of instruction, exhortation and rules for ordinary living. These are set out in this Section.

Note: However a scholarly Muslim has asked to stress that knowledge of God, not the rules for living, is the essence of becoming a true Muslim.

Everyday Religious rules for Muslims

What may not be eaten, unless one is forced by hunger, is one group of these. (Mec. 6/121, 6/142; Mec.16/115; Med. 2/173; Med. 5/3, 5/4; Med. 5/95; Med. 22/77; Med. 30/17).

Prayer rules are indicated fairly generally. (Mec. 11/114; Mec. 4/43; Med. 22/41; Med. 4/101).

'... do not be too loud in your prayer or too quiet, but seek a middle way, (Mec. 17/110).

'So perform the regular prayers in the period from the time the sun is past its zenith till the darkness of the night, and (recite) the Qur'an at dawn ... and during the night wake and pray, as an extra offering of your own. ... Say, "My Lord make me go in truthfully, and come out truthfully, and grant me supporting authority from You." And say, "The truth has come, and falsehood has passed away: falsehood is bound to pass away." (Mec. 17/78).

There are a number of pilgrimage rules and rules on fasting, including for Ramadan. (Mec. 32/15; Med. 2/183; Med. 2/196).

'The faithful have succeeded: those who pray humbly .... (Mec. 23/1).

'... true believers are those whose hearts tremble with awe when God is mentioned, whose faith increases when His revelations are recited to them, who put their trust in their Lord, who keep up the prayer and give to others out of what We (God) provide for them. (Med. 8/2).

'... when you are about to pray, wash your faces and your hands and arms up to the elbows, wipe your heads, wash your feet up to the ankles .... If any of you ... can find no water, then take some clean sand and wipe your face and hands with it. (Med. 5/6).

'He has only forbidden you carrion, blood, pig's meat, and animals over which any name other than God's has been invoked. But if anyone is forced to eat such things by hunger, rather than desire or excess, he commits no sin. God is most merciful and forgiving. (Med. 2/173).

'They ask you again what they should give: say, "Give what you can spare." In this way, God makes His messages clear to you ... (Med. 2/219).

'For men and women who are devoted to God – believing men and women, obedient men and women, truthful men and women, steadfast men and women, humble men and women, charitable men and women, fasting men and women, chaste men and women, men and women who remember God often – God has prepared forgiveness and a rich reward. (Med. 33/35).

Everyday Rules for Commercial dealing

'Whatever you lend out in usury to gain value through other people's wealth will not increase in God's eyes, but whatever you give in charity in your desire for God's approval, will earn multiple rewards. (Mec. 30/39).

'Give full measure, do not sell others short. Weigh with correct scales: do not deprive people of what is theirs. (Mec. 26/181.) Woe to those who give short measure, who demand of other people full measure for themselves. (Mec. 83/1).

'If the debtor is in difficulty, then delay things until matters become easier for him; still, if you were to write it off as an act of charity, that would be better for you, if only you knew. (Med. 2/280).

'You who believe, do not wrongfully consume each other's wealth but trade by mutual consent. (Med. 4/29).

'You who believe, when you contract a debt for a stated term, put it down in writing: have a scribe write it down justly between you. No scribe should refuse to write: let him write as God has taught him, let the debtor dictate, and let him fear God, his Lord, and not diminish (the debt) at all. If the debtor is feeble-minded, weak, or unable to dictate, then let his guardian dictate justly. Call in two men as witnesses. If two men are not there, then call one man and two women out of those you approve as witnesses, so that if one of the two women should forget the other can remind her ... Do not disdain to write the debt down, be it small or large, along with the time it falls due: this way is more equitable in God's eyes, more reliable as testimony, and more likely to prevent doubts arising between you. But if the merchandise is there and you hand it over, there is no blame on you if you do not write it down. Have witnesses present whenever you trade with one another, and let no harm be done to either scribe or witness, for if you did cause them harm, it would be a crime on your part. (Med. 2/282).

In the light of this advice it may be recalled that the City of London has (or had) the expression "an Englishman's word is his bond." This in fact did not arise out of any sense of moral superiority, but from the practical need in quick financial trading to rely on word of mouth. This no longer applies with the existence of internet technology.

'You, who believe, do not consume usurious interest, doubled and redoubled. (Med. 3/130).

'But those of you who take usury will rise up on the Day of Resurrection like someone tormented by Satan's touch. That is because they say, "Trade and usury are the same", but God has allowed trade and forbidden usury. Whoever on receiving God's warning, stops taking usury may keep his past gains – God will be his judge – but whoever goes back to usury will be an inhabitant of the Fire, there to remain. (Med. 2/275).

There are rules relevant to breaking an oath. (Med. 5/89).

Everyday Rules for Wealth and its Distribution

'If anyone desires a harvest in the life to come, We shall increase it for him; if anyone desires a harvest in this world, We shall give him a share of it, but in the Hereafter he will have no share. (Mec. 42/20).

'... do not gaze longingly at what We have given some of them to enjoy, the finery of this present life: We test them through this, but the provision of your Lord is better and more lasting. (Mec. 20/131).

'He (God) provides abundantly or sparingly for whoever He will: ... (Mec. 42/12).

'It is God who gives abundantly to whichever of His servants He will, and sparingly to whichever He will: ... (Mec. 29/62).

'(Nor does He like those) who spend their wealth to show off, who do not believe in Him or the Last Day. (Mec. 4/38)

'The servants of the Lord ... are those who are neither wasteful nor niggardly ... (Mec. 25/62).

'... eat and drink (as We have permitted) but do not be extravagant. (Mec. 7/31).

'Do not gloat .... (Mec. 28/76).

'Do not covet what God has given to some of you more than to others – (Med. 4/32).

'... (Prophet), tell those who hoard gold and silver instead of giving in God's cause that they will have a grievous punishment .... (Med. 9/34).

'Do not eat up your property wrongfully, nor use it to bribe judges, intending sinfully and knowingly to eat up parts of other people's property. (Med. 2/188).

'If you give charity openly, it is good, but if you keep it secret and give to the needy in private, that is better for you .... (Med. 2/271).

Everyday Rules for Social Behaviour

These rules are remarkably modern-sounding for all that having been composed fourteen hundred years or more ago.

'Far better and long-lasting is what God will give to those who ... conduct their affairs by mutual consultation("shura"), give to others out of what We have provided for them; and defend themselves when they are oppressed. (Mec. 42/37).

'Do not turn your nose up at people, nor walk about the place arrogantly, for God does not love arrogant or boastful people. Go at a moderate pace and lower your voice, for the ugliest of all voices is the braying of asses. (Mec. 31/18).

'Say "seek refuge ... against the harm of the slinking whisperer ...." (Mec. 114/4).

'Let harm be requited by an equal harm, though anyone who forgives and puts things right will have his reward from God Himself – He does not like those who do wrong. (Mec. 42/40).

'... if a person is patient and forgives, this is one of the greatest things. (Mec. 42/43).

'Man was truly created anxious .... Not so those ... who give a due share of their wealth to beggars and the deprived; who believe in the Day of Judgment and fear the punishment of their Lord – the punishment of their Lord is not something to feel safe from – who guard their chastity from all but their spouses or their slave girls – there is no blame attached to (relations with) these, but those whose desires exceed this limit are truly transgressors – who are faithful to their trusts and their pledges; who give honest testimony and are steadfast in their prayers. They will be honoured in Gardens of bliss. (Mec. 70/19).

'(The nature of) man is that .... You (people) ... you do not urge one another to feed the poor, you consume inheritance greedily, and you love wealth with a passion. (Mec. 89/15).

'(The servants of the Lord of Mercy are) those who ... when they see some frivolity, pass by with dignity. (Mec. 25/72).

31

'Yet he (man) has not attempted the steep path. What will explain to you what the steep path is? It is to free a slave, to feed at a time of hunger an orphaned relative or a ... poor person in distress (Mec. 90/11).

'They will be given their rewards twice over because they are steadfast, repel evil with good, give to others out of what We have given for them, and turn away whenever they hear frivolous talk, saying, "We have our deeds and you have yours. Peace be with you! We do not seek the company of foolish people." (Mec. 28/54) (Some put-down!).

'Far better and more lasting is what God will give to those ... who shun great sins and gross indecencies, who forgive when they are angry. (Mec. 42/36).

'Do not be tight-fisted, nor so open-handed that you end up blamed and over-whelmed with regret .... Do not strut arrogantly about the earth .... The evil of all these actions is hateful to your Lord. (Mec. 17/29, 37).

'... give their due to the near relative, the needy, and the wayfarer. (Mec. 30/38).

... do not enter people's houses until you have asked permission to do so and greeted those inside .... If you are told, "Go away", then do so .... (Med. 24/27).

'... tell believing men to lower their eyes and guard their private parts. (Med. 24/30).

'And tell believing women that they should lower their eyes, guard their private parts, and not display their charms beyond what (it is acceptable) to reveal .... They should not stamp their feet so as to draw attention to any hidden charms. (Med. 24/31).

'God does not love the conceited, boastful, those who are miserly and who tell other people to be miserly. (Med. 57/24).

'Believers, no group of men should jeer at another, who may after all be better than them; no one group of women should jeer at another who may after all be better than them ... do not use offensive nicknames for one another ... do not spy on one another or speak ill of people behind their backs. (Med. 49/11).

32

'Be good to your parents, to relatives, to orphans, to the needy, to neighbours near and far, to travellers in need, and to your slaves. (Med. 4/36).

'... Do not let hatred of others lead you away from justice. (Med. 5/8).

'... do not give in to the disbelievers and the hypocrites ... God does not put two hearts within a man's breast. (Med. 33/1).

Everyday Rules for Clothing

'(Prophet), tell believing men ... to guard their private parts ... God is well aware of everything they do. And tell believing women that they should ... draw their coverings over their necklines and not reveal their charms except to their husbands, their fathers, their husbands' fathers, their sons, their husbands' sons, their brothers, their brothers' sons, their sisters' sons, their womenfolk, their slaves, such men as attend them who have no sexual desire, or children who are not yet aware of women's nakedness. (Med. 24/30).

Prophet, tell your wives, your daughters and women believers to make their outer garments hang low over them so as to be recognised and not insulted. (Med. 33/59).

No blame will be attached to elderly women who no longer have any desire, if they take off their outer garments without flaunting their charms, but it is preferable for them not to do this .... (Med. 24/60).

Everyday Rules for Family

'... you should be kind to your parents. If either or both of them reach old age with you, say no word that shows impatience with them, and do not be harsh with them, but speak to them respectfully, and lower your wing in humility towards them .... (Mec. 17/23).

'We have commanded man to be good to his parents – his mother struggled to give birth to him; his bearing and weaning took a full thirty months – when he has grown to manhood and reached the age of forty to say, "Lord help me to be truly grateful for Your favours to me and to my parents." (Mec. 46/15).

'Stay well away from the property of orphans except with the best (intentions), until they come of age .... (Mec. 6/152).

'... do not kill your children fearing poverty. We will provide for you and for them" – (Mec. 6/151). (This refers to earlier, pre-Islamic traditional
infanticide.)

There are rules for the care of children, (Med. 2/233), orphans, (Med. 2/220) and widows, (Med. 2/234).

'Believers, your slaves and any who have not yet reached puberty should ask your permission to come in at three times of day: before the dawn prayer; when you lay your garments aside in the midday heat; and after the evening prayer .... When your children reach puberty they should (always) ask your permission to enter, like their elders do. (Med. 24/58).

Rules for Marriage

Note: the rules of dowry, inheritance and consanguinity have not been included in this book.

> The reader can go to the next section when the message of these quotations is clear.

'And do not go anywhere near adultery: it is an outrage, and an evil path. (Mec. 17/32).

'Women have rights similar to their obligations, according to what is fair, and husbands have a degree (of right) over them: (both should remember that) God is almighty and wise. (Med. 2/228).

'You will never be able to treat your wives with equal fairness, however much you may desire to do so, but do not ignore one wife altogether, leaving her suspended (between marriage and divorce) ... but if husband and wife do separate, God will provide for each out of His plenty: He is infinite in plenty and all wise. (Med. 4/129).

'You may marry whichever (other) women seem good to you, two, three or four. If you fear that you cannot be equitable (to them) then marry only one, or your slave(s). (Med. 4/3).

'You may make any of (your women) wait and receive any of them as you wish, but you will not be at fault if you invite one whose turn you have previously set aside: this way it is more likely that they will be satisfied and will not be distressed and will all be content with what you have given them. (Med. 33/51).

'A man can marry a woman of the Book (i.e, a Jew or Christian) and should not make her a mistress. (Med. 5/5).

'If any of you does not have the means to marry a believing free woman, then marry a believing slave – God knows best (the depth of) your faith: you are (all) part of the same family – so marry them with their people's consent and their proper bride-gifts. (Making them) married women, not adulteresses or lovers. (Med. 4/25).

'Do not marry idolatresses until they believe. A believing slave woman, is certainly better than an idolatress. (Med. 2/221).

'Do not give your women in marriage to idolaters until they believe. (Med. 2/221).

'The adulterer is only fit to marry an adulteress or an idolatress, and the adulteress is only (fit) to marry an adulterer or an idolater. (Med. 24/3).

'You who believe, it is not lawful for you to inherit women against their will, nor should you treat your wives harshly, hoping to take back some of the bride-gift you gave them, unless they are guilty of something clearly outrageous. Live with them in accordance with what is fair and kind: if you dislike them, it may well be that you dislike something in which God has put much good. (Med. 4/19).

'Husbands should take good care of their wives, with (the bounties) God has given to some more than to others .... Righteous wives are devout and guard what God would have them guard in their husbands' absence. If you fear high-handedness from your wives, remind them (of the teachings of God), then ignore them when you go to bed, then hit them. If they obey you, you have no right to act against them. (Med. 4/34).

Slavery and Marriage

'Marry off the single among you and those of your male and female slaves who are fit (for marriage). If they are poor, God will provide for them from His bounty: God's bounty is infinite and He is all knowing. Those who are unable to marry should keep chaste until God gives them enough out of His bounty. If any of your slaves wish to pay for their freedom, make a contract with them accordingly, if you know they have good in them, and give them some of the wealth God has given you. Do not force your slave-girls into prostitution, when they themselves wish to remain honourable, in your quest for the short-term gains of this world, although, if they are forced, God will be forgiving and merciful (to them). (Med. 24/32).

Rules for Divorce

'If you (believers) fear that a couple may break up, appoint one arbiter from his family and one from hers. Then if the couple want to put things right, God will bring about reconciliation between them. (Med. 4/35).

'If a wife fears high-handedness or alienation from her husband, neither of them will be blamed if they come to a peaceful settlement, for peace is best. Although human souls are prone to selfishness. (Med. 4/128).

'If you wish to replace one wife with another, do not take back any of her bride-gift even if you have given her a great amount of gold. How could you take it when this is unjust and a blatant sin? How could you take it when you have lain with each other and they have taken a solemn pledge from you? Do not marry women that your fathers married .... This is indeed a shameful thing to do, loathsome and leading to evil. (Med. 4/20).

'Divorce can happen twice, and (each time) wives either be kept on in an acceptable manner or released in a good way. It is not lawful for you to take back anything that you have given (your wives), except where both fear that they cannot maintain (the marriage) within the bounds set by God: if you (arbiters) suspect that the couple may not be able to do this, then there will be no blame on either of them if the woman opts to give something for her release. These are the bounds set by God: do not overstep them. It is those who overstep God's bounds who are doing wrong. (Med. 2/229).

'Divorced women shall have such maintenance as it is considered fair .... (Med. 2/241).

'If they (a slave you have married) commit adultery when they are married, their punishment will be half of that of a free woman. (Med. 4/25). (An interesting concept).

Rules for retribution

'Let harm be requited by an equal harm, though anyone who forgives and puts things right will have his reward from God Himself .... There is no cause to act against anyone who defends himself after being wronged .... (Mec. 42/40).

'... if you (believers) have to respond to an attack, make your response proportionate, but it is best to stand fast. (Mec. 16/126).

'In the Torah (the Jewish Holy Book) We (God) prescribed for them a life for a life, an eye for an eye, a nose for a nose, an ear for an ear ... (etc., etc.,) ... : if anyone forgoes this out of charity, it will serve as an atonement for his bad deeds. (Med. 5/45).

'You who believe, fair retribution is prescribed for you in cases of murder: the free man for the free man, the slave for the slave, the female for the female. But if the culprit is pardoned by his aggrieved brother, this shall be adhered to fairly, and the culprit shall pay what is due in a good way. This is an alleviation from your Lord and an act of mercy. If anyone then exceeds these limits, grievous suffering awaits him. (Med. 2/178).

Personal responsibility for one's circumstances

'Whatever misfortune befalls you (people), it is because of what your own hands have done. (Mec. 42/30).

'Everyone will be ranked according to their deeds and God will repay them in full for what they have done: they will not be wronged. (Mec. 46/19).

'God created the heavens and earth for a true purpose: to reward each soul according to its deeds. (Mec. 45/22).

The reference to "the heavens and the earth" is a reference to life on earth, not a reference to Paradise.

"Bad things happen to good people"

It should be noted that there is no suggestion whatever in the Qur'an that good people may suffer undeserved misfortune; in other words there is absolutely no inkling that "bad things may happen to good people" as puzzled over by Christians, a perspective also illustrated in the Old Testament Book of Job. Job is cited four times in the Qur'an, but never in this context.

There is a section on Predestination, Section 29 on page 78 and a note on page 22.

Rules for The Good Muslim Life

'The servants of the Lord of Mercy are those who walk humbly on the earth, and who, when aggressive people address them, reply, with words of peace; those who spend the night bowed down or standing, worshipping their Lord, who plead, "Our Lord, turn away from us the suffering of Hell, its suffering goes on and on. It is an evil home, a foul resting place!" They are those who are neither wasteful nor niggardly when they spend, but keep a just balance; those who never invoke any other deity beside God, nor take a life, which God has made sacred, except in the pursuit of justice, nor commit adultery. (Mec. 25/63).

'The present life of this world is merely an amusement and a diversion; the true life is in the Hereafter .... (Mec. 29/64).

'Bear in mind that the present life is just a game, a diversion, an attraction, a cause of boasting among you, of rivalry in wealth and children. (Med. 57/20).

The following summation is the most succinct and complete.

'What you have been given is only the fleeting enjoyment of this world. Far better and more lasting is what God will give to those who believe and trust in their Lord; who shun great sins and gross indecencies; who forgive when they are angry; respond to their Lord; keep up the prayer; conduct their affairs by mutual consultation ("shura"); give to others out of what We have provided for them; and defend themselves when they are oppressed. (Mec. 42/36).

"Shura" is referred to a good deal in politics at the present time. However the true significance of "shura" in the Qur'an itself, i.e., "consultation", is seen in the last quotation above, where it is only the sixth of eight precepts for

38

good living, and its context shows that decisions should be made in normal communal life, when associates and neighbours are involved, through mutual consultation. This implies both consulting together and acting in accordance with the conclusions of that consultation.

However, long since the time of the Qur'an, the very few references to "shura" in the Qur'an have been taken as being relevant also to the conduct of national government including government by democratic procedures. The governmental, constitutional contexts of "shura" are discussed in Section 23 on page 45 below, "The Qur'an in a Modern Parliament."

21: Crimes

Nearly all crimes and forbidden acts identified in the Qur'an are only attributed punishment in the form of punishment in Hell. This, of course, has given Muslim polities throughout history wide options for choosing what punishments, man-inflicted, they wish to designate during life for such crimes and forbidden acts. Here is a complete list of all the forbidden acts identified in the Qur'an punishable by human intervention during life on earth.

Over the course of history and in different cultures the nature of these man-designated punishments, should be expected to change. But where earthly punishments are designated in the Qur'an these are binding and unalterable in Islam.

It should be well-noted that stoning is not prescribed for any act or crime in the Qur'an. This of course does not prevent Muslim governments from adopting stoning as a punishment, as in fact was widely done in subsequent history.

The crimes and forbidden acts for which no earthly punishment is designated in the Qur'an are described in Section 16, "Punishments in Hell", and a few in Section 20, "Everyday Rules for Living". For instance no punishment on earth is prescribed in the Qur'an for the sins designated in the Qur'an of blasphemy, apostasy, belief in the Trinity, taking intoxicants, gambling, eating certain foods and lending out in usury.

Thus it is open to a Muslim government to select earthly punishments for these and for the other forbidden acts which have no Qur'anic earthly punishments specified. This, as described in Section 16, means that punishment can be designated by modern Muslim governments, for instance, for drinking intoxicants:

'They ask you (Prophet) about intoxicants and gambling: say, "There is great sin in both, and some benefit for people: the sin is greater than the benefit." (Med. 2/219).

'... do not come anywhere near the prayer if you are intoxicated, ... (Med. 4/43).

Modern Muslim governments have freedom with regard to other wrongful acts for which the Qur'an provides no punishment. (See list on page 15).

In two instances the absence of any earthly punishment in the Qur'an does not negate the earthly effectiveness of the prohibition, because the act itself would be invalid and unenforceable. Thus as usury is forbidden in the Qur'an, this renders usury inherently unenforceable.

In a similar way, the prohibition without an earthly punishment in the Qur'an is effective in the case where marriage to an idolater or idolatress who does not convert and believe in Islam. This bar prevents such a marriage from being legally recognised in a Muslim country. (People of the Book, i.e., Christians, Jews and Zoroastrians are not "idolaters", thus a Muslim man, expressly, may marry a Christian, Jew or Zoroastrian; (Med. 5/5), and nothing says that a Muslim woman, may not marry a Christian, Jewish or Zoroastrian man.)

'Do not marry idolatresses until they believe .... (Med. 2/221).

'... do not give your women in marriage to idolaters until they believe. (Med. 2/221).

An issue which would be debatable in a Muslim country is whether, if any of these forbidden acts were to be accorded punishments by law, should they apply to non-Muslims living in the Muslim country? Presumably, for instance, it is unlikely that food laws would be applied to non-Muslims. The famous statement that there is "no compulsion in religion" (Med. 2/256) should be of weight in these cases. Some prohibitions, however, such as alcohol consumption and gambling, could be rendered punishable crimes for non-Muslims as well as for Muslims on general cultural grounds.

The only forbidden acts in the Qur'an for which the Qur'an itself prescribes an earthly punishment are the following. These forbidden acts should therefore, in accordance with Qur'an, only be punished in the ways prescribed in the Qur'an. These are as follows:

Killing

The earthly consequences of killing another person are covered in the Qur'an in the next two quotations. They provide for private retribution, but do not contemplate governmental execution or imprisonment of the killer:

> '...fair retribution is prescribed for you in cases of murder: the free man for the free man, the slave for the slave, the female for the female. But if the culprit is pardoned by his aggrieved brother, this shall be adhered to fairly, and the culprit shall pay what is due in a good way. (Med. 2/178).

> 'Never should a believer kill another believer, except by mistake. If anyone kills a believer by mistake he must free one Muslim slave and pay
> compensation to the victim's relatives, unless they charitably forego it. If the victim belonged to a people at war with you, but is a believer, then the compensation is only to free a believing slave; if he belonged to a people with whom you have a treaty, then compensation should be handed over to his relatives, and a believing slave set free. (Med. 4/92).

The remaining references to killing do not attach a governmental-administered earthly punishment for murder (or, obviously, killing in battle).

> '... do not kill your children out of fear of poverty." We will provide for you and for them ... (Mec. 6/151), (i.e., infanticide, which was common in Arabia before Muhammad's time.)

> 'Do not take life, which God has made sacred, except by right. (Mec. 6/151).

> 'If you (believers) have to respond to an attack, make your response proportionate, but it is best to stand fast. (Mec. 16/126).

> 'Those who have been attacked are permitted to take up arms because they have been wronged .... (Med. 22/39).

'Fight in God's cause against those who fight you but do not overstep the limits. (Med. 2/190).

'If anyone kills a believer deliberately, the punishment for him is Hell, and there he will remain: ... So you who believe, be careful when you go out to fight in God's way, and do not say to someone who offers you a greeting of peace, "You are not a believer," out of desire for the chance gains of this life (i.e., booty) .... (Med. 4/93).

'Fight them until there is no more persecution, and worship is devoted to God. If they cease hostilities, there can be no (further) hostility, except towards aggressors. (Med. 2/193).

'... you may fight the idolaters at any time, if they first fight you .... (Med. 9/36).

'When you meet disbelievers in battle, strike them in the neck, and once they are defeated, bind any captives firmly – later you can release them as a grace or by ransom – until the toils of war have ended. (Med. 47/4).

Adultery etc.,

The punishments for adultery and other sexual misbehaviour in the Qur'an are as follows:

'Strike the adulteress and the adulterer one hundred times. Do not let compassion for them keep you from carrying out God's law – if you believe in God and the Last Day – and ensure that a group of believers witness the punishment. (Med. 24/2).

'As for those who accuse chaste women of fornication, and then fail to provide four witnesses, strike them eighty times and reject their testimony ever afterwards ...except those who Life on earth repent later and make amends. (Med. 24/4).

'If two men commit a lewd act, punish them both; if they repent and mend their ways, leave them alone – God is always ready to accept repentance .... But God only undertakes to accept repentance from those who do evil out of ignorance and soon afterwards repent .... (Med. 4/16).

'If any of your women commit a lewd act, call four witnesses from among you, then, if they testify to their guilt, keep the women at home until death comes to them or until God shows them another way. (Med. 4/15).

Theft

The punishment for theft is prescribed, but the exemption should be well noted:

'Cut off the hands of thieves whether they are man or woman, as punishment for what they have done, a deterrent from God: God is almighty and wise. But if anyone repents after his wrongdoing and makes amends, God will accept his repentance. (Med. 5/38).

Insurrection against God and Muhammad

The severest earthly punishment in the Qur'an is reserved for insurrection against God and Muhammad (literally presumably dependent on Muhammad's being alive):

'Those who wage war against God and His Messenger and strive to spread corruption in the land should be punished by death, crucifixion, the amputation of an alternate hand and foot, or banishment from the land: a disgrace for them in this world, and then a terrible punishment in the Hereafter, unless they repent before you overpower them – in that case bear in mind that that God is forgiving and merciful. (Med. 5/32).

The above is the full extent of earthly punishment for crimes in the Qur'an. All other forbidden acts are assigned only punishment in Hell. Thus all other Muslim-originated punishments on earth are post-Qur'anic and not specified in the Qur'an.

22: Discrimination in Human Rights for Women

Note:- Some of the citations below have been quoted in other sections of the book.

References to women, children, orphans and slaves are remarkably few in the Qur'an. Women are the primary subject of only about 40 verses out of a total of over 4,700, and most of these are from the Medinan period. This figure does not include verses concerning the details of dowries and divorce, and parenthood in general, nor forbidden degrees of marriage or instructions concerning slavery.

The instances when provisions (other than those concerning dowries, parenthood etc.,) relating to women are discriminatory are:

First, as to marriage,

> 'Wives have rights similar to their obligations, according to what is fair, and (ex) husbands have a degree (of right) over them … (Med. 2/228).

> 'You may marry whichever (other) women seem good to you, two, three, or four. If you fear that you cannot be equitable (to them), then marry only one, or your slave(s): that is more likely to make you avoid bias. (Med. 4/3).

> 'You will never be able to treat your wives with equal fairness, however much you may desire to do so, but do not ignore one wife altogether, leaving her suspended (between marriage and divorce). (Med. 4/129).

After one of Muhammad's wives disclosed something that Muhammad had told her in confidence, it was stated:

> 'His Lord (God) may well replace you with better wives if the Prophet decides to divorce you … " (Med. 66/5)

> 'If you (a husband) fear high-handedness from your wives, remind them (of the teachings of God), then ignore them when you go to bed, then hit them. If they obey you, you have no right to act against them. (Med. 4/34).

As to the last quotation, it should be noted that this action is an obligation not a choice. But in contrast as to a husband it is stated:

> 'If a wife fears high-handedness or alienation from her husband neither of them will be blamed if they come to a peaceful settlement, for peace is best. (Med. 4/128).

Another discriminations is:-

'Concerning your children, God commands you that a son should have the equivalent share of two daughters. (Med. 4/11).

The rules for dower payments can be regarded as unequal. These are not set out in this book.

In divorce there is basic and radical inequality as will be seen in the sub-section on divorce, page 36.

'Prophet, when any of you intend to divorce women … do not drive them out of their homes … either keep them honourably or part with them honourably (Med. 65/1).

'…if you (arbiters) suspect that the couple may not be able to do this, (i.e., maintain the marriage) then there will be no blame on either of them if the woman opts to give something for her release. (Med. 2/229).

But there are specific protections for wives:

'You who believe, it is not lawful to inherit women (i.e., to marry them) against their will, nor should treat your wives harshly, hoping to take back some of the bride-gift you gave them, unless they are guilty of something clearly outrageous. Live with them in accordance with what is fair and kind: if you dislike them, it may well be that you dislike something in which God has put much good. If you wish to replace one wife with another, do not take any of her bride gift back, even if you have given her a great amount of gold. (Med. 4/19).

Women as witnesses have less weight than men but, note, this is only in regard to a contract of sale:

'Call in two men as witnesses. If two men are not there, then call one man and two women out of those you approve as witnesses, so that if one of the two women should forget the other can remind her. (Med. 2/282).

23: The Qur'an in a Modern Parliament

Consultation (shura) is referred to only three times in the Qur'an. The call for "shura" in the Qur'an is generally accepted nowadays as a justification for the practice of democracy in the context of Islam. The three references to shura are usually regarded as those which could give the basis in the Qur'an itself for government by a process of consultation. Thus where the decisions of a democratically elected parliament are put into effect by a government, this is often regarded as affording one manner in which effect can be given to "shura" or consultation. However there is indeed only slight indication of the relevance of "shura" (consultation) used in the Qur'an to matters of government, and the importance of shura has been substantially developed in Islamic thought through thinking which post-dates the Qur'an. The references to consultation, "shura", in the Qur'an are as follows: the first occurs as one point in a general run-down of advice on behaviour applicable to the conduct of communal life ("conduct their affairs"): this Meccan reference inherently calls for the conclusions of any consultation to be put into effect by those concerned in them. However "conduct their affairs" strongly suggests that the contemplated subject-matter of the consultation is personal agreements in the ordinary course of business and living. The statement is:

> 'Far better and more lasting is what God will give to those who believe and trust in their Lord; who shun great sins and gross indecencies; who forgive when they are angry; respond to their Lord; keep up the prayer; *conduct their affairs by mutual consultation ("shura")*, give to others out of what We have provided for them; and defend themselves when they are oppressed. (Mec. 42/36). (author's italics)

A further two references to "shura", not relevant, are found at Medina 2/233 and concern consultation between parents when agreeing on suckling and weaning their child.

The fourth and only other reference to "shura", consultation, in the Qur'an concerns a description of the advice which God is shown as giving to Muhammad after a mishap in a battle in Medina against the Meccans when, in order to avoid the risk that his followers would desert him, God advises him to consult with his followers.

This is however the only express reference which relates "shura" to governmental affairs. It clearly limits "consultation" to a process taking place prior to Muhammad himself making his own decision in the matter, after the conclusion of his consultation with the people of Medina. It looks very like a recommendation by God to Muhammad to employ a little "realpolitik". It is clear from the text that Muhammad was faced with a very real public relations challenge from followers who were in a rebellious frame of mind and considering abandoning Muhammad.

> 'By an act of mercy from God, you (Prophet) were gentle in your dealings with them – had you been harsh, or hard-hearted, they would have dispersed and left you – so pardon them and ask for forgiveness for them. Consult with them about matters, then, when you (Muhammad) have decided on a course of action, put your trust in God. (Med. 3/159).

It looks a little as if in down-to-earth politics it might have been more a question of asking forgiveness *from* them, rather than asking forgiveness *for* them.

Thus, according to this precedent, so far as government-related consultation is concerned, it should be confined to consultation with the population by the leader which will not necessarily determine the nature of the leader's subsequent action. "Shura" in the Qur'an therefore only bears a loose relationship with the issues of modern democracy.

Modern Muslim Attitudes

In considering the application of the Qur'an to a modern-day democracy in a Muslim-majority country, a Report: *'Muslim Grassroots in the West Discuss Democracy'* (http://muslim-grass-roots-discuss-democracy.com and http://www.unaoc.org) may be of interest, reporting the views of round-table discussion groups across Britain and the USA of lay Muslims living in these two countries in 2005 and 2006. The study has subsequently been followed up in 2009 to 2015 with discussion groups of lay Muslims in Canada, Germany, France, Italy and Spain. The results of these later discussions were *identical* with those conducted in 2005 and 2006 in Britain and the USA. This is particularly remarkable as the later discussions took place before, during and after the political upheavals of the "Arab Spring".

Lay Muslims living in the West in fact are the only class of ordinary people in the world who have practical and personal cognisance of both Islam and of Western democracy. This is a remarkable point and worthy of real emphasis and consideration.

For the purpose of the above discussions, democracy was defined as comprising the election of representatives by one person one vote, (and was not to include "one person one vote, one time"), secret ballot, the government to follow the views of the majority of the elected representatives, and protection of minorities. The last condition was included because substantial minorities, which may not hope ever to govern, exist in many Muslim-majority countries. Though this drawback is lessened if coalition government as suggested below is adopted.

Indeed successful development of democracy in Muslim countries may well come to depend on the effectiveness of coalition governments in Muslim countries with substantial minorities, as this ensures that all interests feel that they "own" the government and the constitution. This appears at the present time to be the chief message of the first practical consequences of the "Arab Spring", when one contrasts the recent developments in Tunisia with those, for instance, in Egypt.

In fact the hoped-for propensity of Muslim majority countries for generally acceptable governments to be based on coalitions of the various interests could be the greatest contribution of Islam to modern government.

All these discussions of ordinary lay Muslims living in the West showed that, for the Muslims in those discussions, democracy was considered compatible with Islam but with the one proviso that "nothing contrary to the Qur'an shall happen" in a notional Muslim-majority democratic country. For this reason, all statements in the Qur'an which might be relevant to the question "what is contrary to the Qur'an?" are relevant in a modern Muslim country where democratic government is concerned.

These statements in the Qur'an have been set out in the **Sections, 21, Crimes: A Complete List of All the Forbidden Acts Punishable During Life on Earth Identified in the Qur'an, and Section 22, Discrimination in Human Rights for Women,** so that non-Muslim readers can see for themselves what constraints on the working of democracy in a modern Muslim- majority democracy the Qur'an contains. From these citations it will be seen that statements in the Qur'an which should limit the freedom of a democratic legislator are, *except as regards to women's rights*, very limited.

It is of interest that in the lay Muslim discussions mentioned above, Muslims in the West universally regarded democracy as merely a technology of government, not as an ideal or principle, as it is often considered to be by non-Muslim Westerners.

"Nothing contrary to the Qur'an shall happen."

Of course, a number of concepts in the Qur'an acceptable in the seventh century AD may no longer be regarded as politically viable. Notable among these would be the acceptance of slavery. The Qur'an does not call for slavery; it is however no doubt debatable whether the acceptance of the existence of slavery in the Qur'an prevents a political agreement nowadays not to employ slavery in today's world.

Regardless of the legalistic position of slavery in the Qur'an, the charitable stance of the Qur'an is clear.

'Yet he has not attempted the steep path. What will explain to you what the steep path is? *It is to free a slave*, to feed at a time of hunger an orphaned relative .... (Mec. 90/12). (Author's italics)

Another issue to which the same considerations are relevant is that of polygamy, which is legitimate in the Qur'an though a number of modern Muslim-majority countries have indeed legislated against polygamy.

24: Slavery

This paragraph is only included because of the mass slavery imposed on the women and children of the Yazidis, and indeed apparently other women, by ISIS. Slavery is recognised as acceptable and normal in the Qur'an. It is however not required as an institution by the Qur'an, and though the Qur'an is regarded as the timeless word of God and thus might be considered to impose a bar to express abolition of slavery in a Muslim state, it has in fact been legislated against in a number of Muslim states, e.g., Qatar, the Yemen and Saudi Arabia.

The dreadful treatment of the Yazidi women and children as slaves by ISIS is totally different from the treatment indicated in the Qur'an, where references to slavery tend to indicate a humane benign attitude. On slavery and marriage, see page 36.

25: Relations with Christians and Jews

Although the Qur'an often regards Christians and Jews as semi-allies of Muslims ("People of the Book"), Jews are also often criticised for failing to follow the Torah and to accept the lead of Muhammad and the Qur'an, and Christians for regarding Jesus as the Son of God. The latter is possibly rendered more significant because of the exhortations in the Qur'an to fight against the pagans of Mecca who are condemned as polytheists for worshipping 'partners' of God, sometimes referred as 'daughters' of God. Much of the zeal shown in the Qur'an in the Meccan, that is the earlier suras, was fired by the emphasis on condemnation of the worship of more than one god.

It will be noted that when Christian belief in the Son of God is in mind, the attitude in the Qur'an to Christians is uncompromisingly hostile. Indeed the Christian simultaneous belief in monotheism and the Trinity – "One God: Father, Son and the Holy Spirit", calls for considerable mental robustness on the part of Christians, and renders Trinity Sunday sermons the least popular amongst Christian clergy who have to write and deliver them.

> '(Believers), argue only in the best way with the People of the Book, except with those of them who act unjustly. Say, "We believe in what was revealed to us and in what was revealed to you, our God and your God is one (and the same); we are devoted to Him." (Mec. 29/46).
>
> 'The (Muslim) believers, the Jews, the Christians, and the Sabians (a certain monotheistic group); all those who believe in God and the Last Day and do good – will have their rewards with their Lord. (Med. 2/62).
>
> 'You (Prophet) are sure to find that the most hostile to the believers are the Jews and those (note: this is not a reference to Christians) who associate other deities with God; you are sure to find that the closest in affection towards the believers are those who say, "We are Christians", for there are among them people devoted to learning and ascetics. These people are not given to arrogance, and when they listen to what has been sent down to the Messenger, you will see their eyes overflowing with tears because they recognise the Truth (in it). They say, "Our Lord, we believe, so count us among the witnesses. Why should we not believe in God and in the Truth that has come down to us …? For saying this, God has rewarded them with Gardens graced with flowing streams …." (Med. 5/82).

Despite the clearly sympathetic and favourable attitude shown in the last quotation, when the Christian "Son of God" and the Trinity are in consideration, the Qur'an is implacable:–

'Those (i.e., Christians) who say "God is the Messiah, son of Mary" have defied ... God .... If anyone associates others with God, God will forbid him from the Garden and Hell will be his home. (Med. 5/72).

'The Jews said "Esra is the son of God," and the Christians said "the Messiah is the Son of God" .... May God thwart them. (Med. 9/30).

'... the Messiah, Jesus, son of Mary, was nothing more than a messenger of God, His word, directed to Mary, and a spirit from Him. So believe in God and his messengers. And do not speak of a "Trinity" – stop (this), that is better for you – God is only one God, He is far above having a son .... (Med. 4/171).

'Those (i.e., Christians) who say that God is the third of three are defying (the truth): there is only One God. If they persist in what they are saying, a painful punishment will afflict those of them who persist .... The Messiah, son of Mary, was only a messenger; other messengers had come and gone before him; his mother was a virtuous woman; both ate food (like other mortals). See how clear We make these signs for them: see how deluded they are. (Med. 5/73).

In addition there is also one general hostile statement concerning Christians even when the Trinity is not expressly given as grounds for hostility, though this statement may have the Trinity in mind.

Fight those of the People of the Book who do not (truly) believe in God and the Last Day, who do not forbid what God and His Messenger have forbidden, who do not obey the rule of justice, until they pay the tax and agree to submit. (Med. 9/29).

The Life of Jesus

The Qur'an covers a few aspects of Jesus' life in some detail.

'The angels said, "Mary, God gives you news of Word from Him, whose name will be the Messiah, Jesus, son of Mary, who will be held in honour in this world and the next, who will be one of those brought near to God. He will speak to people in his infancy and in his adulthood. He will be one of the righteous." She said, "My Lord, how can I have a son when no man has touched me?" (The angel) said, "This is how God creates what He will; when He has ordained something, He only says, 'Be' and it is ... He will send him as a messenger to the Children of Israel." I have come to you with a sign from your Lord: I will make the shape of a bird for you out of clay ... (Med. 3/45).

'Jesus, son of Mary, said, "Children of Israel, I am sent to you by God, confirming the Torah that came before me, and bringing good news of a messenger to follow me whose name will be Ahmad." (The name "Ahmad" is related to the name Muhammad). Yet when he came to them with clear signs, they said, "This is obviously sorcery." (Med. 61/6).

'... As Jesus, son of Mary, said to the disciples, "Who will be my helpers in God's cause?" The disciples said, "We shall be God's helpers." Some of the Children of Israel believed and some disbelieved. We supported the believers against their enemy and they were the ones who came out on top. (Med. 61/13).

'These are the revelations of God which We recite to you (Muhammad) with the truth, and you truly are one of the messengers. We favoured some of these messengers above others. God spoke to some: others he raised in rank; We gave Jesus, son of Mary, Our clear signs and strengthened him with the Holy Spirit. If God had so willed their successors would not have fought each other after they have been brought clear signs. But they disagreed: some believed and some disbelieved. If God had so willed, they would not have fought each other, but God does what He will. (Med. 2/252).

Although the attitude in the Qur'an to the wholly and solely manhood nature of Jesus is clear, the Qur'an accepts the resurrection or ascension of Jesus and his virgin birth, and rejects the crucifixion.

'The People of the Book (i.e., the Jews) said "We have killed the Messiah, Jesus, son of Mary, Messenger of God." They did not kill him, nor did they crucify him, though it was made to appear like that to them; those that disagreed about him are full of doubt, with no knowledge to follow, only supposition; they certainly did not kill him – No! God raised him up to Himself ... (Med. 4/157).

Curious elaborations concerning Jesus

The Qur'an appears also to have had some obscure Christian sources, possibly among local Christians in the desert.

When the disciples said, "Jesus, son of Mary, can your Lord send down a feast to us from heaven?" ... They said, "We wish to eat from it; to have our hearts reassured; to know that you have told us the truth; and to be witnesses of it". Jesus, son of Mary, said, "Lord, send down to us a feast from heaven so that we can have a festival ... a sign from You ...." God said, "I will send it down to you, but anyone who disbelieves after this will be punished ...." (Med. 5/112).

Curious aspects in the life of the Virgin Mary are described.

'She withdrew from her family to a place to the east and secluded herself away; We sent Our Spirit to appear before her in the form of a normal human ... he said, I am but a Messenger from your Lord, (come) to announce to you the gift of a pure son. She said, "How could I have a son when no man has touched me. I have not been unchaste," and he said, "This is what your Lord said: 'It is easy for Me – We shall make him a sign to all people, a blessing from Us.' ... " She withdrew to a distant place and, when the pains of childbirth drove her to (cling to) the trunk of a palm tree, she exclaimed, "I wish I had been dead and forgotten long before all of this!" but a voice cried to her from below, "Do not worry: your Lord has provided a stream at your feet and, if you shake the trunk of the palm tree towards you, it will deliver fresh ripe dates for you, so eat, drink, be glad, and say to anyone you may see: 'I have vowed to the Lord of Mercy to abstain from conversation, and I will not talk to anyone today.' " (Mec. 19/16).

'On the Day when God assembles all the messengers and asks, "What response did you receive?" They will say, "We do not have that knowledge: You alone know things that cannot be seen." Then God will say, "Jesus, son of Mary! Remember my favour to you and to your mother: how I strengthened you with the Holy Spirit, so that you spoke to people in your infancy, and as a grown man; how I taught you Scripture and wisdom; the Torah, and the Gospel; how by My leave you fashioned the shape of a bird out of clay, breathed into it, and it became, by My leave, a bird; how by My leave, you healed the blind person and the leper; how by My leave, you brought the dead back to life; how I restrained the Children of Israel from (harming) you when you brought them clear signs, and those of them who disbelieved, said, 'This is clearly nothing but sorcery.' " (Med. 5/109).

'When God says, "Jesus, son of Mary, did you say to people, 'Take me and my mother as two gods alongside God?' he will say, 'May You be exalted! I would never say what I had no right to say – ... You know all that is within me, though I do not know what is within You. You alone have full knowledge of things unseen ... Ever since You took my soul, You alone have been the watcher over them (the People)...' " (Med. 5/116).

26: Muhammad Governs Medina in a Time of War

As will have been seen from the sections above, the Medina suras provide a substantial part of the religious message of the Qur'an. But in addition the Medina suras are particularly interesting because they show how Muhammad is described as having built up and maintained an orderly life in Medina for his fellow Muslims in their new town and refuge after they were described as having fled from Mecca to Medina. He is shown as organising city government, the defence of the city and the welfare of its inhabitants in its domestic, public and religious activities and establishing rules on all aspects of life.

Muhammad is shown also as conscious of the need to give the lead, by example, in their domestic life, having to galvanise them to defend the city and fight a strong enemy, the Meccans, in the hardest form of warfare, apparently a civil war among hitherto closely related people. It will be seen that Muhammad sometimes is seen as having considerable difficulty in mastering the inhabitants of Medina. The selections below are specifically related to the matters of government seen as arising in Medina.

There is no description in the Qur'an of Muhammad sharing the powers of government with others, though he is shown as carrying out consultation, "shura", with the citizens on one recorded occasion before, he, Muhammad is himself shown to make his own decision. This is referred to in the last quotation under "Governmental Actions" on page 61 below (Med. 3/159).

The Medinan suras are most particularly notable as showing Muhammad himself actually being linked directly with God in forty or more verses in which "God and His Prophet/Messenger' jointly lead, decide, warn, encourage and judge in regard to the activities of the citizens of Medina. Thus instructions for the behaviour of the Muslim inhabitants of Medina, preparation for battle etc., are linked, remarkably, to God and his Messenger jointly. Historically, politically and theologically this concept is unique. Typically, for instance:

'Whoever obeys the Messenger obeys God. (Med. 4/80).

Exhortations to Show Respect for Muhammad Consonant with Respect for God

Muhammad is shown as claiming respect for himself consonant with that which he exhorts for God. This rather extraordinary claim, which might be regarded practically as twin-ship with God, is clear from the following quotations.

'True believers are those who believe in God and His Messenger, who, when they are gathered with him on a communal matter, do not depart until they have asked his permission – those who ask your permission (Prophet) are the ones who truly believe in God and His Messenger (Med. 24/62).

'(People), do not regard the Messenger's summons to you like one of you summoning another – God is well aware of those of you who steal away surreptitiously – and those who go against his order should beware lest a trial afflict them or they receive a painful torment. (Med. 24/63).

'Those who pledge loyalty to you (Prophet) are actually pledging loyalty to God Himself. (Med. 48/10)

'God was pleased with the believers when they swore allegiance to you (Prophet) under the tree. (Med. 48/18).

'By your Lord, they will not be true believers until they let you (Muhammad) decide between them in all matters of dispute, and find no resistance in their souls to your decisions, accepting them totally .... (Med. 4/65).

'... If anyone opposes God and His Messenger, God punishes them severely – "That is what you get! Taste that! – and the torment of Fire awaits the disbelievers." (Med. 8/13).

'Believers, do not push yourselves forward in the presence of God and His Messenger ... (Med. 49/1).

'... Believers, do not raise your voices above the Prophet's, do not raise your voice when speaking to him as you do to one another ... It is those who lower their voices in the presence of God's Messenger whose hearts God has proved to be aware – they will have forgiveness, and a great reward – but most of those who shout to you (Prophet) from outside your private rooms lack understanding. It would have been better for them if they had waited patiently for you to come out to them; but God is all forgiving and merciful. (Med. 49/2).

'Those who oppose God and His Messenger will be brought low ....
(Med. 58/5).

'There are others who insult the Prophet by saying, "He will listen to
anything ...." An agonising torment awaits those who insult God's
Messenger .... Do they not know that whoever opposes God and His
Messenger will go to the Fire of Hell and stay there? ... (Med. 9/61).

'Whoever obeys God and the Messenger will be among those He (God)
has blessed. (Med. 4/69).

'When God and His Messenger have decided on a matter that
concerns them, it is not fitting for any believing man or woman to
claim freedom of choice in the matter. (Med. 33/36).

'If they (inhabitants of Medina who abandoned faith and rejected the
Muslim faith) turn (on you), then seize and kill them wherever you
encounter them. (Med. 4/89).

Instances of Opposition from Muslims in Medina

There are several instances of opposition among Muslims in Medina under
attack by Meccan polytheists, ranging from minor back-biting to open
hostility to Muhammad and these are apparent in many of the Medinan
Suras. It is clear that Muhammad is seen to have had no easy time governing
Medina:

> The reader can go to the next section when the message of
> these quotations is clear. However the full list of quotations
> is, it must be confessed, remarkably engaging.

'(Some people) say, "We believe in God and the Messenger
(Muhammad), we obey," but then some of them turn away ... and
when they are summoned to God and His Messenger in order for
him (Muhammad) to judge between them, some of them turn away
.... Do they fear that God and His Messenger might deal with them
unjustly? ... When the true believers are summoned to God and His
Messenger in order for him (Muhammad) to judge between them, they
say, "We hear and we obey." These are the ones who will prosper;
whoever obeys God and His Messenger, stands in awe of God, and
keeps his duty to Him will be triumphant .... Say, "obey God, obey
the Messenger ...." (Med. 24/47).

56

'(Prophet) you can see the hostility on the faces of the disbelievers when Our (God's) messages are recited clearly to them: it is almost as if they were going to attack those who recite Our (God's) messages to them .... (Med. 22/72).

'God and His angels bless the Prophet – so, you who believe, bless him too and give him greetings of peace. Those who insult God and His Messenger will be rejected by God in this world and the next – He has prepared a humiliating torment for them – and those who undeservedly insult believing men and women will bear the guilt of slander and flagrant sin. (Med. 33/56).

'Believers, obey God and His Messenger (Muhammad): do not turn away when you are listening to him; do not be like those who say, "We heard," though in fact they were not listening .... (Med. 8/20).

'Remember (Prophet) when the disbelievers plotted to take you captive, kill, or expel you. They schemed and so did God: He is the best of schemers. Whenever Our Revelation is recited to them they say, "We have heard all this before – we could say something like this if we wanted – this is nothing but ancient fables." They also said "God, if this is really the truth from You, then rain stones on us from the heavens, or send some other painful punishment." But God would not send them punishment while you (Prophet) are in their midst. (Med. 8/30). (A very literalistic comment.)

'If the hypocrites, the sick at heart, and those who spread lies in the city do not desist, We (God) shall rouse you (Prophet) against them, and then they will only be your neighbours in this city for a short while. They will be rejected. Wherever they are found they will be arrested and put to death. (Med. 33/60).

'The hypocrites fear that a sura will be revealed exposing what is in their hearts – say, "Carry on with your jokes ..." yet if you were to question them, they would be sure to say, "We were just chatting, just amusing ourselves." Say, "Were you joking about God, His Revelations and His Messenger?" (Med. 9/64).

'Some of these people listen to you (Prophet), but, once they leave your presence, they sneer at those who have been given knowledge, saying, "What was that he just said?" These are the ones whose hearts God has sealed, those who follow their own desires. (Med. 47/16).

'Whoever obeys the Messenger (Muhammad) obeys God. If some pay no heed … They say, "We obey you," but as soon as they leave your presence some of them scheme by night to do other than what you said. (Med. 4/80).

'Have you not seen how those who have been forbidden to hold secret conversations go back afterwards and hold them, and conspire with one another in what is sinful, hostile and disobedient to the Messenger (Muhammad)? When they come to you they greet you with words God has never used to greet you, and say inwardly: "Why does God not punish us for what we say?" Hell will be punishment enough for them: they will burn there – an evil destination. You who believe, when you converse in secret, do not do so in a way that is sinful, hostile and disobedient to the Messenger, but in a way it is good and mindful (of God). (Med. 58/8).

'This is how it is: Here you are, you love them but they do not love you … They say, "We believe," but when they are alone they bite their fingertips in rage at you, (Prophet), say, "Die of rage (if you wish)!" (Med. 3/119)

'… If anyone opposes God and His Messenger, God punishes them severely – "That is what you get! Taste that! " – and the torment of the Fire awaits the disbelievers. (Med. 8/13)

'When they meet the believers, they say, "We believe," but when they are alone with their evil ones, they say, "We're really with you; we were only mocking." (Med. 2/14).

Cowardice in Medina

> The reader can go to the next section when the message of these quotations is clear. However, once again the full list of quotations is remarkably engaging.

'… Only those who do not have faith in God and the Last Day ask your permission to stay at home (from fighting). … (Med. 9/45)

'They would only have given you trouble if they had gone out with you (to battle): they would have scurried around, trying to sow discord among you … . (Med. 9/47)

'... Their wealthy ask you permission, (to be exempt from fighting) saying, "Allow us to stay behind .... " (Med. 9/86)

'... When a decisive sura that mentions fighting is sent down, you can see the sick at heart looking at you (Prophet) visibly fainting at the prospect of death. (Med. 47/20)

'When fighting was ordained for them, some of them feared men as much as, or even more than, they feared God, saying, "Lord, why have You ordained fighting for us? If only You would give just a little more time." (Med. 4/77).

'They would only have given you trouble if they had gone out (to battle) with you: they would have scurried around, trying to sow discord among you, and some of you would willingly have listened to them,... but if misfortune comes your way, they will say to themselves, "We took precautions for this" – and go away rejoicing. (Med. 9/47).

'Those who were left behind were happy to stay behind when God's Messenger set out; they hated the thought of striving in God's way with their possessions and their persons. They said to one another, "Do not go (to war), in this heat." Say, "Hellfire is hotter." If only they understood! Let them laugh a little; they will weep a lot in return for what they have done. So (Prophet), if God brings you back to a group of them, who ask you for permission to go out (to battle), say, "You will never go out and fight an enemy with me: you chose to sit at home the first time, so remain with those who stay behind now." (Med. 9/81).

'... only those who do not have faith in God and the Last Day ask your permission to stay at home; they have doubt in their hearts and so they waver. (Med. 9/45).

'When a sura is revealed (saying), "Believe in God and strive hard alongside His Messenger" their wealthy ask your permission (to be exempt) .... (Med. 9/86).

'The ones open to blame are those who asked you for exemption despite their wealth ... (Med. 9/93).

'They would certainly have followed you (Prophet) if the benefit was within sight and the journey short, but the distance seemed too great for them. (Med. 9/42).

'You who believe, remember God's goodness to you when mighty armies massed against you. We (God) sent a violent wind and invisible forces against them. God sees all that you do. They massed against you from above and below, your eyes rolled (with fear), your hearts rose into your throats, and you thought (ill) thoughts of God. There the believers were sorely tested and deeply shaken: the hypocrites and the sick at heart said, "God and His Messenger promised us nothing but delusions!" Some of them said, "People of Yathrib (old name for Medina) you will not be able to withstand (the attack), so go back!" Some of them asked the Prophet's permission to leave, saying, "Our houses are exposed," even though they were not – they just wanted to run away: had the city been invaded from all sides, and the enemy invited them to rebel, they would have done so almost without hesitation. Yet they had already promised God that they would not turn tail and flee, and a promise to God will be answered for. (Prophet), say, "Running away will not benefit you. If you manage to escape death or slaughter, you will only be permitted to enjoy (life) for a short while ..." God knows exactly who among you hinder others, who (secretly) say to their brothers, "Come and join us," who hardly ever come out to fight, who begrudge you (believers) any help. When fear comes, you (Prophet) see them looking at you with eyes rolling like someone in their death throes; when fear has passed, they attack you with sharp tongues and begrudge any good. (Med. 33/9).

Personal relations of Muhammad with family and followers

Muhammad became upset over an incident concerning his wife, A'isha:

'When you heard the lie, (a slander on A'isha, his wife) why did believing men and women not think well of their own people and declare; "This is obviously a lie?" And why did the accusers not bring four witnesses to it? If they cannot produce such witnesses, they are liars in God's eyes. If it were not for God's bounty and mercy towards you in this world and the next, you would already have been afflicted by terrible suffering for indulging in such talk. ... you thought it was trivial, but to God it was very serious. When you heard the lie, why did you not say, "We should not repeat this – God forbid! – it is a monstrous slander."? God warns you never to do anything like this again, if you are true believers. (Med. 24/12).

Muhammad has to assert his status in Medina:

Believers, if a troublemaker brings you news, check it first, in case you wrong others unwittingly ... and be aware that it is God's Messenger who is among you ... in many cases you would certainly suffer if he (Muhammad were to follow your wishes.) (Med. 49/6).

'Believers, do not enter the Prophet's apartments for a meal unless you are given permission to do so; do not linger until (a meal) is ready. When you are invited, go in; then when you have taken your meal, leave. Do not stay on and talk, for that would offend the Prophet, though he would shrink from asking you to leave ... When you ask his wives for something, do so behind a screen: this is purer for both your hearts and for theirs. It is not right for you to offend God's Messenger, just as you should never marry his wives after him: that would be grievous in God's eyes. (Med. 33/53).

'Wives of the Prophet, if any of you does something clearly outrageous, she will be doubly punished – ... but if any of you is obedient to God and His Messenger and does good deeds, know that We (God) shall give her a double reward. (Med. 33/30).

'Wives of the Prophet you are not like any other woman ... speak in an appropriate manner; stay at home, and do not flaunt your finery as they used to in the pagan past ... (Med. 33/32).

'Prophet, tell your wives, your daughters and women believers to make their outer garments hang low over them so as to be recognised and not insulted. (Med. 33/59).

'When God and His Messenger have decided on a matter that concerns them, it is not fitting for any believing man and woman to claim freedom of choice in the matter. (Med. 33/36).

Disrespectful Behaviour Towards Muhammad in the City

This sometimes happened when a trading caravan or entertainment arrived in the city and provides a very personal touch.

'... they scatter towards trade or entertainment whenever they observe it and leave you (Prophet) standing there. Say, "What God has is better than any entertainment or trade: God is the best provider." (Med. 62/9).

Governmental Actions: Pledging Loyalty; Decision Making

'When God and His Messenger have decided on a matter that concerns them, it is not fitting for any believing man or woman to claim freedom of choice in the matter: whoever disobeys God and His Messenger is far astray. (Med. 33/36).

'By your Lord, they will not be true believers until they let you decide between them in all matters of dispute, and find no resistance in their souls to your decisions, accepting them totally – if we had ordered, "Lay down your lives" or "Leave your homes," they would not have done so, except for a few – it would have been far better for them … if they had done as they were told … (Med. 4/65).

'… if anyone opposes the Messenger (Muhammad), after guidance has been made clear to him, and follows a path other than that of the believers, We (God) shall leave him on his chosen path – We shall burn him in Hell, an evil destination. (Med. 4/115).

'Those who pledge their loyalty to you, (Prophet), are actually pledging loyalty to God Himself – God's hand is placed on theirs – … (Med. 48/10).

This refers to people placing their hands under Muhammad's to pledge loyalty.

'God was pleased with the believers when they swore allegiance to you (Prophet) under the tree: He knew what was in their hearts and so He sent tranquillity down to them and rewarded them with a speedy triumph and with many future gains. (Med. 48/18).

'Believers do not push yourselves forward in the presence of God and His Messenger (Muhammad) … do not raise your voices above the Prophet's, do not raise your voice when speaking to him as you do to one another … It is those who lower their voices in the presence of God's Messenger whose hearts God has proved to be aware – and they will have forgiveness. (Med. 49/1).

'Out of an act of mercy from God, you, Prophet, were gentle in your dealings with them – had you been harsh, or hard-hearted, they would have dispersed and left you – so pardon them and ask for forgiveness for them. Consult with them about matters, then, when you (Muhammad) have decided on a course of action, put your trust in God. (Med. 3/159).

This group of quotations infers the necessity of authoritarian government in a time of emergency, but the last of these also underlines the prudence of maintaining the acquiescence of the believers through consultation with them by Muhammad *before* he, by himself, makes his own decisions. This procedure of Muhammad making a decision alone after consulting the people can be contrasted with the merits of "conducting your affairs by consultation" (which clearly means making *joint* decisions *in consultation*) discussed in the last paragraph of Section 20 "Everyday Rules for Living as a Muslim" (see page 27 above) in a pre-war Meccan sura (Mec. 42/36). See also Section 23 on page 45, "The Qur'an in a Modern Parliament."

Distribution of Funds and War Booty

'They ask you, (Prophet), about (distributing) the battle gains. Say, "That is a matter for God and His Messenger" ... (Med. 8/1).

'Know that one fifth of your battle gains belongs to God and the Messenger (Muhammad). (Med. 8/41).

'So enjoy in a good and lawful manner the things you have gained in war. (Med. 8/69).

'When you (believers) set off somewhere that promises war gains, those who (previously) stayed behind will say, "Let us come with you" ... But tell them (Prophet) "You may not come with us." (Med. 48/15).

'Among you there is the sort of person is sure to lag behind: if calamity befalls you, he says, "God has been gracious to me that I was not there with them," yet he is sure to say, if you are favoured by God, "If only I had been with them, I could have made great gains,". (Med. 4/72).

Cowardice and Bravery

There are exhortations to defend Medina and to fight in the war against the Meccans:

> The reader can go to the next section when the message of these quotations is clear

'Fight in God's cause against those who fight you, but do not overstep the limits: God does not love those who overstep the limits. Kill them wherever you encounter them, and drive them out from where they drove you out. (Med. 2/190).

'Fighting is ordained though you dislike it. You may dislike something although it is good for you. (Med. 2/216).

'They will not stop fighting you (believers) until they make you revoke your faith, if they can. If you revoke your faith ... you will be inhabitants of the Fire, there to remain. (Med. 2/217).

'Prophet, urge the believers to fight: if there are twenty of you who are steadfast, they will overcome two hundred, and a hundred of you, if steadfast, will overcome a thousand of the disbelievers .... (Med. 8/65).

'Believers, when you meet a force in battle, stand firm and keep God firmly in mind, so that you may prosper. Obey God and His Messenger, and do not quarrel with one another, or you may lose heart and your spirit may desert you. (Med. 8/45).

'If they turn (on you), then seize them and kill them wherever you encounter them ... (Med. 4/89).

'So if they neither withdraw, nor offer you peace, nor restrain themselves from fighting you, seize and kill them wherever you encounter them. (Med. 4/91).

'... If you do not go out and fight, God will punish you severely and put others in your place. (Med. 9/39).

'And there is no blame attached to those who come to you (Prophet), for riding animals and to whom you said, "I cannot find a mount for you:" they turned away with their eyes overflowing with tears of grief that they had nothing that they could contribute. (Med. 9/92).

'The Lord has answered them: "I will not allow the deeds of any one of you to be lost, whether you are male or female, each is like the other (in rewards). I will certainly wipe out the bad deeds of those who emigrated (to Medina) and were driven out of their homes (in Mecca), who suffered harm for My cause, who fought and were killed. I will certainly admit them to Gardens graced with flowing streams, as a reward from God: the best reward is with God." (Med. 3/195).

'But if they (God's enemies and yours) incline towards peace, you (Prophet) must also incline towards it. (Med. 8/61).

Treatment of Traitors

'If the hypocrites, the sick at heart, those who spread lies in the city do not desist, We shall rouse you, (Prophet) against them, and then they shall only be your neighbours in the city for a short while. They will be rejected wherever they are found. They will be arrested and put to death. This has been God's practice with those who went before. (Med. 33/60)

Conclusion on the War in Medina

The Meccan supporters of Muhammad who fled to Medina from Mecca (their hometown) were very often disloyal to Muhammad in his war defending Medina from the Meccan attacks. But eventually he prevailed against the Meccans despite all the failings of his followers to fully support him. But the Qur'an shows that internal opposition to Muhammad was constantly a weakness among his supporters which he had to overcome.

27: "Jihad"

The word "Jihad" is so frequently referred to nowadays in the media in the context of war, fighting and terrorism, that it is desirable to evaluate the uses of it in the Qur'an itself. "Jihad" has a number of meanings in English according to context. In the Qur'an it occurs some 40 times, with a few duplications. The word "Mujahideen" is similar in meaning to "Jihad". They are marked with an asterisk in the quotations below.

In view of the current ubiquitous references to "Jihad" in the press, it is important to see the word in its true Qur'anic setting.

Some uses of the word "Jihad" or "Mujahideen" refer primarily to living a conscientious Muslim life, and some to supporting Muhammad and his rule in Medina. Some refer to emigrating from Mecca to Medina to support Muhammad there with the implication of fighting the Meccans. The rest clearly refer to fighting in defence of Medina against the disbelieving Meccans. They are called on to fight with their "possessions and their lives" under Muhammad's command. No uses refer to fighting anyone except in defence of Medina against the Meccans. The conclusion, when taking the wording at its face value, must be that in the Qur'an the word "Jihad" when contemplating fighting is *only* used to refer to defensive fighting in the cause of the Medinans in Medina. There is no expressed or suggested projection onto future wars. But of course to Muslims for whom the Qur'an is the timeless word of God, it is permissible to attempt to apply its statements to any situation including the wars of today.

(i) "Jihad" as Probably Primarily Meaning "Striving" in One's Life to Do God's Will in General

The quotations from Mecca are the more likely to be pacific, as they predate the war in Medina.

Quotations from Mecca

'Those who exert* themselves do so for their own benefit – God does not need His creatures. (Mec. 29/6, The word "Jihad" occurs twice).

'We have commanded people to be good to their parents, ... If they strive* to make you associate with Me, anything about which you have no knowledge, then do not obey them. (Mec. 29/8). Similarly (Mec. 31/15).

'... so (Muhammad) do not give in to the disbelievers: strive* hard* against them with this Qur'an. (i.e., by reciting, this Qur'an.) (Mec. 25/52; The word "Jihad" occurs twice).

'But We shall be sure to guide to Our (God's) ways those who strive* hard* for Our cause: God is with those who do good. (Mec. 29/69).

'But to those who leave their homes after persecution then strive* and remain steadfast, Your Lord will be most forgiving and most merciful. That will be on the Day when every soul will come pleading for itself, when every soul will be paid in full for all its actions and they will not be wronged. (Mec. 16/110).

Note: this quotation comes from the Meccan verses before the emigration to Medina and the war there, despite the reference to leaving one's home which is a little surprising. In Medina all Muslims had gone there, leaving their original home.

Quotations from Medina

'It is they (the disbelievers and the hypocrites) who criticise the believers who give freely and those who can only give a little with great* effort*: they scoff at such people, but it is God who scoffs at them. (Med. 9/79).

This clearly refers to moral support, not to fighting.

'Strive* hard* for God as is His due: He has chosen you and placed no hardship in your religion, the faith of your father Abraham. (Med. 22/78; The word "Jihad" occurs twice).

'We shall test you to see which of you strive* your hardest and are steadfast; We shall test the sincerity of your assertions. (Med. 47/31). (The word "Mujahideen" is used.)

The last two quotations could refer to striving to do God's will in general or to fighting.

'Prophet, strive* against* the disbelievers and the hypocrites, (among his fellow inhabitants of Medina), and be tough with them. (Med. 9/73).

This seems to refer to Muhammad disciplining his own citizens in Medina, rather than to fighting the Meccans.

(ii) References of Indefinite Import, Most Probably Having Fighting In Mind

'But those who have believed, migrated and striven* for* God's cause, it is they who can look forward to God's mercy. (Med. 2/218).

'Do you consider giving water to pilgrims and tending the Sacred Mosque to be equal to the deeds of those who believe in God and the Last Day and who strive* in* God's path? (Med. 9/19). This presumably compares non-military activities with military ones.

(iii) The following Jihad References as Likely as Not to Envisage the Possibility of Fighting

'Did you think you would enter the Garden without God first proving which of you would struggle* for* His cause and remain steadfast? (Med. 3/142).

'Say (Prophet), "If your fathers, sons, brothers, wives, tribes, the wealth you have acquired, the trade which you fear will decline, and the dwellings you love are dearer to you than God and His Messenger and the struggle* in* His cause, then wait until God brings about His punishment." God does not guide those who break away. (Med. 9/24).

'You who believe, be mindful of God, seek ways to come closer to Him and strive* for* His cause, so that you may prosper. (Med. 5/35).

'You who believe, if any of you go back on your faith, God will soon replace you with people He loves and who love Him, people who are humble towards the believers, hard on the disbelievers, and who strive* in* God's way without fearing anyone's reproach. (Med. 5/54).

'Do you think that you will be left untested without God identifying which of you will strive* for* His cause and take no supporters apart from God, His Messenger and other believers? (Med. 9/16).

(iv) Passages Referring to Jihad Positively Implying the Possibility of Fighting:

There are similar but shorter passages concerning Meccans emigrating from Mecca to support Muhammad in Medina which presumably have fighting in mind such as:

'... if you truly emigrated in order to strive* for* My (God's) cause and seek My good pleasure ....." (Med. 60/1).

(v) Passages Referring to Jihad Clearly Describing Medinans Actually Fighting Meccans with Their Persons:

'So go out, no matter whether you are lightly or heavily armed, and struggle* in* God's way with your possessions and your persons. (Med. 9/41).

'Those believers who stay at home, apart from those with an incapacity, are not equal to those who commit themselves and their possessions to striving* in* God's way. (Med. 4/95) ("Mujahideen", word occurs twice).

'Those who believed and emigrated (to Medina) and struggled* for* God's cause with their possessions and persons, and those who gave refuge and help, are all allies of one another. (Med. 8/72).

'Those who believe, who migrated and strove* hard* in God's way with their possessions and their persons, are in God's eyes much higher in rank; it is they who will triumph .... (Med. 9/20).

'Those who ... do not ask you for exemption from struggle* with their possessions and their persons .... (Med. 9/44).

'But the Messenger and those who believe with him strove* hard* with their possessions and their persons. (Med. 9/88).

'The true believers are the ones who have faith in God and His Messenger and leave all doubt behind, the ones who have struggled* with their possessions and their persons in God's way: they are those who are true. (Med. 49/15).

'Those who were left behind were happy to stay behind when God's Messenger (Muhammad) set out; they hated the thought of striving* in God's way with their possessions and their persons. They said to one another, "Do not go out (to war) in this heat". (Med. 9/81).

'Those who believed and emigrated, and struggled* for* God's cause, and those who gave refuge and help – they are the true believers and they will have forgiveness and generous provision. And those who came to believe afterwards, and emigrated and struggled* alongside you, they are part of you .... (Med. 8/74).

As a reasonable conclusion it may be said that it is notable that all the Medinan references to Jihad are to fighting which is concurrent with and relevant to the apparent time of the statement to which it is directed, i.e., during the war between Medina and Mecca in which the Meccans were the original aggressors. This is the natural meaning in the Qur'an. In other words in the Qur'an "Jihad" is, in so far as it relates to fighting, directed at defensive fighting to protect the Medinans from attack.

However, it should be warned that by taking an extreme aggressive reading, it would be said that the Jihad described here is only illustrative and the message for the reader is not to be tied to the particular circumstances envisaged in the statements. On this basis present day Muslims cannot be deterred from applying the statements in the Qur'an to their present day conflicts, so long as they are fighting enemies who they consider to be enemies of God. This unfortunately franks Sunni and Shia fighting each other and ISIS fighting all (including Muslims) who do not support ISIS, BUT it does NOT frank the killing of captives for which ISIS has proudly become known.

28: ISIS Beheadings and Mass Killings

This section is directed particularly to the beheadings and other means of killing war captives and individual hostages held by ISIS (Islamic State in Iraq and Syria) and the mass killing by them of Yazidis, Shia Muslims, Christians and others in Iraq and Syria. It is also relevant to the wider instructions that have been given to ISIS supporters everywhere in the world to kill military and civilian inhabitants in the 60 or more states which are allied against ISIS. This attitude franks the attacks in Paris, Brussels and Berlin.

The projected victims include Muslims living in those states who are not Sunni and Sunnis who do not support ISIS.

Some of these statements have been quoted in earlier sections but are repeated to ensure that all "killing" statements in the Qur'an are to be found in this Section.

ISIS Killing of Civilian and Military Prisoners and Muslims who do not Support ISIS

On the 23rd September 2014 *'The Times'* reported that ISIS had declared that in addition to killing non-ISIS military and civilians in Iraq and Syria, Muslim ISIS supporters living in the West should "carry out self-starter attacks on Western soldiers and civilians in retaliation for air strikes on its (ISIS) fighters in Syria and Iraq .... Attacks could be carried out with rocks, knives, poison or running someone over with a car ...."

> 'If you can kill a disbelieving American or European – especially the spiteful and filthy French – or an Australian or Canadian, or any other disbeliever from the disbelievers waging war, including citizens of the countries that entered into a coalition against the Islamic State,[1] then rely upon Allah, and kill him in any manner or way however it may be.'

In other words anyone in the world who is not an ISIS believer, regardless of their religion is designated as a possible target to be killed.

---

[1]Presumably this means the USA, Canada, Britain, France, Germany, Australia, Austria, Turkey, Russia, the Syrian government, Jordan, Saudi Arabia, Qatar, the Emirates, Iraq, Iran and Bahrain.

'Do not ask for anyone's advice and do not seek anyone's verdict. Kill the disbeliever whether he is civilian or military, for they have the same ruling. Both of them are disbelievers. Both of them are considered to be waging war'.

The "disbeliever", of course separates Muslims from non-Muslims in the Qur'an. In the ISIS context here, however, it would presumably include all (including Muslims) who do not support ISIS itself.

Supporters of ISIS were told to use whatever they could find to attack everyone other than ISIS supporters in countries that have supported the US-led campaign against Islamic State.

The statement continued:

'If you are not able to find an IED (improvised explosive device) or a bullet, then single out the disbelieving American, Frenchman or any of their allies. Smash his head with a rock, or slaughter him with a knife, or run him over with your car, or throw him down from a high place, choke him or poison him'.

'If you are unable to do so, then burn his home, car, or business, or destroy his crops. If you are unable to do so, then spit in his face. *If yourself refuses to do so*, while your brothers are being bombarded and killed, and while their blood and wealth everywhere is deemed lawful by the enemies, *then review your religion.*"(Author's italics).

Conclusion

This is a call to Muslims to support a very broad interpretation of the Qur'an, notably that all the world, *including non-ISIS Muslims*, is condemned and worthy of death at the hands of ISIS and permanent punishment in Hell, except the ISIS Sunnis, and also that it is meritorious to kill Muslim and non-Muslim prisoners.

Surely an Unintendedly Misleading Assertion

Tom Holland, a renowned historian, is quoted in *'The Times'* of 29 September 2014 as saying:

'The claim that Islamic State (ISIS) ideology has nothing to do with Islam was wishful thinking, and that the militants' theology had a strong basis in the Koran and early Islamic history.'

Tom Holland continues:

> 'The grim truth is that sanctions can be found in the Koran, in the biographies of Muhammad and in the histories of early Islam for much that strikes the outside world as most horrific about Islamic State (ISIS).'

This is a somewhat misleading statement for those unfamiliar with the Qur'an.

In response to Tom Holland it can be said that the essential point is that only the Qur'an is universally accepted as the actual word of God by Muslims and is therefore unchallengeable in the Muslim mind. It should be noted that Tom Holland does not allege that anything in the Qur'an itself justifies anything "horrific". Certainly nothing in the Qur'an franks the killing of prisoners. Tom Holland's failure to note this is remarkable to say the least.

It is the other Muslim documents to which he refers which "contain every kind of horror" and which raise genuine problems. But none of these documents is accepted by all the various strains of Islam, nor are any of them accepted by any Muslims as being the direct word of God and therefore unchallengeable. Needless to say, in addition, very many of these other documents contradict each other.

Tom Holland therefore does a serious injustice to the Qur'an itself by not making it clear that the Qur'an is not on the same footing as the other documents to which he refers. In fact as this book shows there is little approaching horror regarding treatment of humans in the actual words of the Qur'an itself, nor that its contents are, as he implies, "horrific".

It will be accepted over the course of time that the origins of the present text of the Qur'an are more complex than at present is assumed by Muslims. However whatever the origins are, it is the precise wording of the existing text of the Qur'an as it is accepted at the present time that is taken by Muslims to be the word of God. Tom Holland by implication besmirches this text.

In Answer to Tom Holland: What the Qur'an Actually Says;

The specific enemies in the Qur'an in all cases were in fact the non-Muslim fighters from Mecca who attacked Medina, the town to where Muhammad and his supporting Muslims had fled. These non-Muslims were generally polytheists.

All that the Qur'an says of "killing" is set out below. Some references have already been quoted under Jihad because some of the Jihad quotations above in Section 27 imply or call for killing. They are repeated here for completeness.

(i) Four References in the Qur'an to Killing Enemies

These refer to those who attack Muhammad's Muslims first during actual fighting i.e., clearly defensive killing (Author's italics throughout).

> 'They would dearly like you to reject faith, as they themselves have done, to be like them. So do not take them as allies until they migrate (to Medina) for God's cause. *If they turn (on you)*, then seize and kill them wherever you encounter them. Take none of them as an ally or supporter. (Med. 4/89).

> 'You will find others who wish to be safe from you, and from their own people, but whenever they are back in a situation where they are tempted (to fight you), they succumb to it. So if they neither withdraw, nor offer you peace, *nor restrain themselves from fighting you*, seize and kill them whenever you encounter them: We give you clear authority against such people. (Med. 4/91).

> 'Those who *wage war against God and His Messenger* and strive to spread corruption in the land should be punished by death, crucifixion, the amputation of alternate hand and foot, or banishment from land. (Med. 5/33).

> 'Fight in God's cause against those who fight you, but do no overstep the limits. God does not love those that overstep the limits. Kill them whenever you encounter them and drive them out *from wherever they drove you out* ... Fight them until there is no more persecution and worship is devoted to God. If they cease hostilities there can be no further hostility *except towards aggressors* .... So if anyone commits aggression against you attack him as he attacked you. (Med. 2/190).

Confirming the defensive character of these calls to fighting is the following comment:–

> 'But if they incline to peace, you (Prophet) must also incline towards it and put your trust in God. (Med. 8/61)

73

(ii) Two Quotations that imply Muhammad's Muslims were defending themselves

'Their Lord has answered them: 'I will not allow the deeds of any one of you to be lost, whether you are male or female, each is like the other (in rewards). I will certainly wipe out the bad deeds of those who emigrated and *were driven out of their homes*, who suffered harm for My cause, who fought and were killed. I will certainly admit them to the Gardens graced with flowing streams, as a reward from God: the best reward is with God.' (Med. 3/195). (Author's italics.)

'(Believers), fight them *until there is no more persecution*, and all worship is devoted to God alone. (Med. 8/39). (This suggests a defensive response.)

(iii) Four further exhortations in the Qur'an to kill

Here it is not stated whether or not the enemy attacks the Muslims first. These therefore include offensive killing.

'When the (four months) are over, wherever you encounter the idolaters, kill them, seize them, besiege them, wait for them at every lookout point; but if they repent, maintain the prayer, and pay the prescribed alms, let them go on their way, for God is most forgiving and merciful. If any of the idolaters should seek your protection (Prophet), grant it to him so he may hear the Word of God. (Med. 9/5).

'When you meet the disbelievers in battle, strike them in the neck, and once they are defeated, bind any captives firmly – later you can release them as a grace or for a ransom – until the toils of war have ended. (Med. 47/4).

'God has purchased the persons and possessions of the believers in return for (i.e., as a price for entering) the Garden (Paradise) – they fight in God's way: they kill and are killed. (Med. 9/111).

'It was God's will to establish the truth according to His word and to finish off the disbelievers. (Med. 8/7).

(iv) Three instances where the killing of enemies is attributed directly to God

'... it was God's will to establish the truth according to His Word and to finish off the Disbelievers .... (Med. 8/7).

'It was not you who killed (the enemy) but God. (Med. 8/17).

'I am with you: give the believers firmness" ... and if anyone opposes God and His Messenger, God punishes them severely – "That is what you get! Taste that!" – and the torment of the Fire awaits the disbelievers. (Med. 8/12).

It should be well noted that none of these references to killing suggest killing enemies who have been captured or have surrendered, and give no ground, however widely the Qur'an could justifiably be "interpreted", for ISIS executions.

(v) Five Encouragements to Fight Defensively in God's Cause Without Actually Mentioning Killing

These next six quotations are clear case of a *response* to an attack. The subsequent sixteen could envisage aggressive or defensive fighting.

'So if anyone commits aggression against you, attack him if he attacked you, but be mindful of God, and know that He is with those who are mindful of Him. (Med. 2/194).

'If you (believers) have to respond to an attack, make your response proportionate, but it is best to stand fast. (Mec. 16/126).

'God decrees that there are twelve months – ordained in God's Book on the Day when He created the heavens and earth – four months are sacred ... Do not wrong yourselves in these months – though you may fight the idolaters at any time, if they first fight you ... (Med. 9/36).

'How could you not fight a people who have broken their oaths, who tried to drive the Messenger out, who attacked you first? .... Fight them: God will punish them at your hands. (Med. 9/13).

'Where the believers are concerned, they (the disbelievers) respect no tie of kinship or treaty. They are the ones who are committing aggression .... If they repent, keep up the prayer and pay the prescribed alms then they are your brothers in faith .... But if they break their oaths after having made an agreement with you and revile your religion, then fight these leaders of disbelief – oaths mean nothing to them .... (Med. 9/10).

(vi) Seventeen references to Fighting Where it is Not Stated to be Defensive

'Why should you not fight in God's cause for those oppressed men, women and who cry out 'Lord, rescue us from this town whose people are oppressed!' (Med. 4/75).

'The worst creatures in the sight of God are those who reject Him and will not believe ... If you meet them in battle, make a fearsome example of them to those who come after them, so that they may take heed .... Prepare against them whatever forces you (believers) can muster including war horses to frighten off (these) enemies of God and of yours .... If they incline towards peace you (Prophet) must also incline towards it. (Med.8/55).

'So go out no matter whether you are lightly or heavily armed, and struggle in God's way with your possessions and your persons. (Med. 9/41).

'Fight in God's cause and remember that He is all hearing and all knowing. (Med. 2/244).

'Say (Prophet) fight in God's way. You are accountable only for yourself. Urge the believers on. (Med. 4/84).

'(Believers), fight them until there is no more persecution, and all worship is devoted to God above: if they desist, then God sees all they do, but if they pay no heed, be sure God is your protector. (Med. 8/29).

'Those who believed and emigrated (from Mecca to Medina) and struggled for God's cause with their possessions and persons and those who gave refuge and help, are all allies of one another. (Med. 8/72).

'Fight those of the People of the Book who do not (truly) believe in God in the last Day, who do not forbid what God and His Messenger have forbidden, who do not obey the rule of justice.(Med. 9/29).

'If you do not go out to fight, God will punish you severely and put others in your place. (Med. 9/39).

'Prophet strive hard against the disbelievers and the hypocrites. Deal with them sternly. (Med. 66/9).

'People, urge the believers to fight: if there are twenty of you are steadfast, they will overcome two hundred. (Med. 8/65).

'Fight them until there is no more persecution, and all worship is devoted to God alone. (Med. 8/39).

'Go out whether you are lightly or heavily armed, and struggle in God's way with your possessions and your persons. (Med. 9/41).

'(Prophet) do you not see those who were told, "Restrain yourselves from fighting, perform the prayer, and pay the prescribe alms? When fighting was ordained for them, some of them feared men as much as, or more than, they feared God, saying, 'Lord, why have you ordained fighting for us? If only you would give us a little more time!' " (Med. 4/77).

'Believers, when you meet the disbelievers in battle, never turn your backs on them; if anyone does so on such a day – unless manoeuvring to fight or join a fighting group – he incurs the wrath of God. (Med. 8/15).

'Do not be faint-hearted in pursuing the enemy: if you are suffering hardship, so are they. (Med. 4/104).

'Those who believe, who migrated and strove hard in God's way with their possessions and their persons, are in God's eyes much higher in rank. (Med. 9/20).

Conclusion

The "killing" and "fighting" statements in the Qur'an are limited in number and all clearly are referable to Muhammad's war with Mecca. If one reads the Qur'an as a historical record this is the conclusion that will be arrived at, and no more.

If one regards the Qur'an as timeless (as Muslims do) some of the above quotations could be called upon as referable to conflicts that took, and take, place after the reception of the Qur'an. This can give ground for middle-of-the-way Muslims to rely on the above quotations by analogy to encourage, guide and instruct them in current religious conflicts. But it cannot be undeniably alleged that the Qur'an expressly countenances them, as those concerned must show that their enemies are recognised as such in the Qur'an or in consequence to what the Qur'an says.

So far as ISIS is concerned some of the above quotations could arguably be taken as direct instructions to kill those (including Muslims) who do not believe in concurrence with their particular views. This is despite the fact that nowhere is killing war captives countenanced in the Qur'an.

29: Predestination

There is little intimation, and certainly no emphasis on the possibility of predestination in the Qu'ran, but see the comments on page 22 above and the quotations there referred to. Some of these quotations are capable of indicating predestination. They are not repeated here because they do not appear to be deliberate, undoubted assertions of predestination. And the quotations below, of closest relevance, more basically reflect the comprehension of God's all-seeing eye. Certainly there is no sense of human helplessness deriving from predestination. The following are the closest brushes with the concept. (Italics are the author's).

'It is He who calls your souls back by night, knowing what you have done by day, then raises you up again in the daytime until your *fixed term* is fulfilled. (Mec. 6/60).

'It is God who created you from dust and later from a drop of fluid; then he made you into two sexes; no female conceives or gives birth without His knowledge; no person grows old or has his life cut short, *except in accordance with a Record*: all this is easy for God. (Mec. 35/11).

'We made the night and day as two signs ... the daylight for seeing ... to know how to count the years and calculate. We have explained everything in detail. We have *bound each human being's destiny to his neck*. On the Day of resurrection We shall bring out a record for each of them, which they will find spread out wide open. (Mec. 17/12).

'God takes souls at the time of the death and the souls of the living while they sleep – He keeps hold of those whose death He has ordained and sends the others back *until their appointed time*. (Med. 39/42).

'No soul may die except with God's permission at a *predestined time.* (Med. 3/145).

'They say, "If we had had our say in this, none of us would have been killed here." Tell them "Even if you had resolved to stay at home, those who *were destined to be killed* would still have gone out to their deaths." (Med. 3/154).

'There is an *appointed term* for every community, and when it is reached they can neither delay or hasten it, even for a moment. (Mec. 10/49).

'There is a *time set for every people*: they cannot hasten it, nor, when it comes, will they be able to delay it for a single moment. (Mec. 7/34).

These last two statements should only to be considered as illustrative of the destruction of wicked communities, not of individuals. See also Section 14 on page 13 above.

30: The Concept of Evolution

The many descriptions of the creation of the skies, the earth and its contents and its animal inhabitants in the Qu'ran are neutral in the light of later concepts of evolution; while in on the other hand there are statements in the Old Testament (as distinct from the New Testament) which taken literally directly conflict with this concept.

The same can be said, indeed, with regard to the literal Old Testament statements concerning the creation of mankind. For instance in the Qur'an, Woman (Eve) is not made from Man (Adam); and though the Garden of Eden is referred to, man's expulsion from it by God is not described as "The Fall," and there is no statement that man was created immortal but fell from this to mortality because of sin. God's creation of man from clay, a drop of liquid etc. is frequently referred to.

31: Some Striking Stand-Alone Statements

As pointed out earlier most statements in the Qur'an are repeated many times at intervals throughout the Book. But there are certain statements which occur only once or occasionally twice, without elaboration or immediate context, and which are of inherent significance. These are all consonant with tenets set out in this book, but they afford interesting vignettes.

From Mecca

1. We God do not burden any soul with more than it can bear. (Mec. 23/62). (Similarly Med. 2/286).

2. No soul can believe except by God's will and He brings disgrace on those who do not use their reason. (Mec. 10/99).

3. Repel evil with good. (Mec. 23/96).

4. It is God who gives abundantly to whichever of His servants He will, and sparingly to whichever He will. (Mec. 29/62).

5. We (God) send devils to incite disbelievers to sin. (Mec. 19/83).

6. Let harm be requited by an equal harm though anyone who forgives and puts things right will have his reward from God himself. (Mec. 42/40).

7. If all the trees on earth were pens and all the seas, with seven more seas besides (were ink), still God's words would not run out .... (Mec. 31/27). Similarly, Mec. 18/109.

From Medina

8. People, We created you from a single man and a single woman and made you into races and tribes so that you should recognise one another. (Med. 49/13).

9. Life in this world is only a game, a pastime. (Med. 47/338).

10. The present world is only an illusory pleasure. (Med. 3/185).

11. God presents this illustration: a slave controlled by his master, with no power over anything, and another man We have supplied with good provision, from which he gives alms privately and openly. Can they be considered equal? ... God presents another illustration: two men, one of them dumb, unable to do anything, a burden to his carer – whatever task he directs him to, he achieves nothing good – can he be considered equal to one who commands justice and is on the straight path? (Med. 16/75).

12. The (disbelievers) schemed but God also schemed; God is the Best of Schemers. (Med. 3/54).

13. We (God) decreed to the Children of Israel that if anyone kills a person – unless in retribution for murder or spreading corruption in the land – it is as if he kills all mankind, while if anyone saves a life it is as if he saves the lives of all mankind. (Med. 5/32).

14. … do not contribute to your destruction with your own hands …. (Med. 2/195). (This is said to refer to suicide.)

15. On that Day, people will come forward in separate groups to be shown their deeds: whoever has done an atom's weight of good will see it, but whoever has done an atom's weight of evil will see that. (Med. 99/6).

16. There is no compulsion in religion: so true guidance has become distinct from error, so whoever rejects false gods and believes in God has grasped the firmest handhold, one that will never break. God is all hearing and all knowing. God is the ally of those who believe; He brings them out of the depths of darkness and into the light. As for the disbelievers, their allies are false gods who take them from the light into the depths of darkness, they are inhabitants of the Fire …. (Med. 2/256).

17. Say (Prophet), "Disbelievers: I do not worship what you worship, you do not worship what I worship, I will never worship what you worship, you will never worship what I worship: you have your own religion and I have mine." (Med. 109/1).

18. He (God) doubles any good deed and gives a tremendous reward of His own. (Med. 4/40).

19. A kind word and forgiveness is better than a charitable deed followed by hurtful (words). (Med. 2/263).

20. Hold fast to God's rope all together; do not split into factions. (Med. 3/103).

About the Author

Amédée Turner is a Queen's Counsel and was a Member of the European Parliament from 1979 until 1994.

The original motivation for this book arose when he was a member of the Advisory Council to the Anglican Observer at the United Nations, being moved to run a campaign to study lay Muslim attitudes to Western democracy. He organised some fifty round table discussions with more than 700 lay Muslims discussing the relationship between Islam and Western democracy. These discussions took place in the USA, Britain, Canada, Germany, Italy, France and Spain in the period 2005 to 2015, thus preceding, during and after the "Arab Spring".

Index

Printed in Great Britain
by Amazon